D1332756

Martin Steffens

K. F. SCHINKEL

TASCHEN

HONG KONG KÖLN LONDON LOS ANGELES MADRID PARIS TOKYO

Illustration p. 2 ▶ Karl Friedrich Schinkel, portrait by Johann Eduard Wolff, 1820.
Illustration p. 4 ▶ Detail of the Old Museum

To stay informed about upcoming TASCHEN titles, please request our magazine at www.taschen.com/magazine or write to TASCHEN America, 6671 Sunset Boulevard, Suite 1508, USA–Los Angeles, CA 90028, contact-us@taschen.com, Fax: +1-323-463 4442. We will be happy to send you a free copy of our magazine which is filled with information about all of our books.

© 2003 TASCHEN GmbH
Hohenzollernring 53, D-50672 Köln
www.taschen.com

Edited by ▶ Peter Gössel, Bremen
Project manager ▶ Swantje Schmidt, Bremen
Design and layout ▶ Gössel und Partner, Bremen
Translation ▶ David Blair, Johannes Molthan and Jutta Ziegler, Bodenheim

Printed in Germany
ISBN 978-3-8228-2760-4

Contents

Introduction

Casino in Klein-Glienicke, Berlin-Wannsee, interior view of the central room, 1824/25.
Klein-Glienicke Castle was reconstructed by Schinkel, and was owned by Prince Charles of Prussia. Schinkel's design of the casino situated in the park was based on an idea by Crown Prince Frederick William. The architect was actively involved in the reconstruction work of all the Prussian princes' country seats.

Karl Friedrich Schinkel (1781–1841) is perhaps the best-known German architect, having left an indelible mark on the artistic era of the first half of the 19th century, subsequently also known as the "Schinkel era." However, he was not only an architect—he also painted and worked as a general designer, stage designer, art writer and royal building authority official. The most varied creative talents were united in this one individual; and he succeeded in putting them to good use thanks to his inherent self-discipline, organisational talent and determination. As a universally active artist, he came to be regarded as the definitive authority on art and taste—not only in the then Kingdom of Prussia, but way beyond.

The turbulent political landscape of the time might also provide some background to Schinkel's artistic life history and his phases of activity in various artistic genres. During Napoleon's occupation of Prussia (1806–13), Schinkel worked mainly as an artist—there were no building contracts available. As Prussia was regaining its strength after the wars of liberation, Schinkel rose to the status of "state architect", although he never officially carried this title. He accomplished nearly all of his artistic work during the reign of King Frederick William III (1797–1840), who repeatedly made his influence felt on Schinkel's state building designs. Schinkel also regularly worked for the Prussian royal family. In this capacity, he was actively responsible for the alterations and furnishings of the Berlin Prince's Palaces and the royal country estates. Event-ually, the sought-after architect was even "loaned out" to foreign sovereigns for design projects such as palaces in the Crimea and on the Acropolis. As a member of the senior building commission (Oberbaudeputation), which he headed from 1830 onwards, he was finally responsible for all important church and state building projects

Casino in Klein-Glienicke, view from the riverside, 1824/25.
The casino with its terraces and pergolas opens out to the river. The castle is set back into the park so far that the traveller approaching on the river or from Potsdam on Glienicke Bridge first sees the cubic structure of the casino.

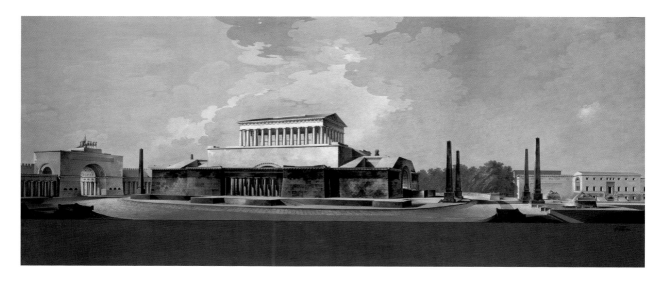

Design for monument to Frederick II, drawing by Friedrich Gilly, 1797.
The design by Friedrich Gilly, who was to become Schinkel's teacher and friend, is what triggered Schinkel's wish to become an architect while he was still at school. Later, he would frequently use features of Gilly's works as a reference.

in Prussia. His name is also tied to the introduction of the preservation of monuments and historic buildings as a duty of the state in Prussia.

Karl Friedrich Schinkel was born in the town of Neuruppin on March 13, 1781. His father was the superintendent of the garrison town in the Mark of Brandenburg. In 1787, the family lost their home in a disastrous fire that ravaged the town. When the father died following pneumonia soon afterwards, Schinkel's mother moved into the preachers' widows' home with her children. In 1794, she decided to relocate to the capital, mainly with her children's education in mind. Once in Berlin, Schinkel entered grammar school, but apart from showing some talent for the arts, he was a mediocre pupil. An important inspiration came to Schinkel on his visit to the 1796 Academy Exhibition. Amongst other exhibits, he saw a design for a monument to Frederick the Great by the architect Friedrich Gilly. Supposedly, it was this impression that formed his decision to become an architect. Schinkel referred to Gilly's design in his later works – especially in his plans for a memorial cathedral. Schinkel left grammar school early to join the Gilly household, where he started as the Gillys' apprentice in all but name. David Gilly, the experienced architectural theorist and master builder, laid the foundations for Schinkel's thorough apprenticeship. Friedrich, who was only nine years Schinkel's senior, became his mentor and friend. Schinkel copied drawings that Friedrich Gilly had brought back to Berlin from his study travels, thus familiarising himself with the most modern architecture of the day. He also took an active part in the Gillys' construction works. When Schinkel enrolled as a pupil at the newly founded General School of Architecture (the Academy of Architecture), he had already gathered a wealth of experience in architectonics. In his apprenticeship period, he occupied himself with at least the theoretical aspects of all the building projects that he would later work on in his career as an architect—even as a pupil, he designed stage scenery and public buildings such as museums and theatres.

Schinkel's mother and his friend, Friedrich Gilly, both died in 1800. All at once, the young man was alone in the world. He left the Academy of Architecture to finish the architectural projects that his friend had started. He completed his training just four years after his initial decision to become an architect. His first independent work was the Pomona Temple (Pomonatempel), a tea pavilion on Potsdam's Pfingstberg, in 1801.

In 1803, Schinkel reached the age of majority and thus gained access to his small inheritance. He invested it in a study visit lasting almost two years and taking him to Bohemia, Austria, Italy and Sicily, as well as France. Schinkel returned to Berlin in 1805. There was, however, little in the way of lucrative architectural work there at that time; Prussia was preparing for war. Schinkel still used every opportunity to make a name for himself as an artist—he took part in a competition to design a monument to Martin Luther in 1805. After Prussia was defeated by Napoleon's army in 1806, construction came to a standstill in the whole country. The ambitious young architect did not have any prospect of applying his abilities until 1815. Schinkel therefore made use of his talent as a painter to cover his essential costs of living. Sketches he had made in Italy served as a basis for elaborate, all-round panoramas and "visual perspective illustrations," some of which were extremely large in size; others referred to current events— for example, the 1812 Great Fire of Moscow. Although Schinkel had never actually trained as a painter, he gained a reputation as a skilful artist, with his works publicly exhibi-

Schinkel in Naples, painting by Franz Louis Catel, 1824
This portrait was painted on Schinkel's second journey to Italy. It shows the architect in his quarters with a view of the Gulf of Naples.

ted either in huts or rented rooms. He was also successful with his romantic landscapes and architectural paintings. Schinkel could cover his own costs and, soon afterwards, even sustain a family from the entrance charges to his exhibitions and from the sale of paintings. He married Susanne Berger in 1909, a marriage that resulted in three children. There is little known about Schinkel's private life from his own accounts—the private individual mostly took second place to the public official and artist of genius.

In 1809, Schinkel also made the royal couple's acquaintance through his diorama exhibitions. Shortly afterwards, he was consulted for the decoration work on some of the rooms in the royal residence, the Crown Princes' Palaces (Kronprinzenpalais). He was finally appointed to the civil service as an official in the building authority in 1810 on the recommendation of Wilhelm von Humboldt. Humboldt, the then head of the Prussian educational system, had met Schinkel in Rome in 1803. Schinkel worked as a royal building authority official until his death. He made a living, but his income was not enough to support an extravagant lifestyle. On the other hand, Schinkel tended to remain within society's norms, not living as a bohemian or bon viveur. In fact, he made the impression of an untiring worker and conscientious servant of the state and the royal family. Still, the building authority official had hardly any possibilities for architectural activity in the initial years due to the unfavourable political climate.

After the death of Queen Louise, Schinkel prepared a design for her mausoleum in 1810. He may not have had any chance of seeing his design implemented, but Schinkel

The Palermo panorama, around 1808.
In perspective distortion, the etching shows the painted panorama that Schinkel had erected in front of St Hedwig's Cathedral in Berlin. This may have been the design for an advertising leaflet.

New Pavilion, also called Schinkel Pavilion, in the Castle grounds in Charlottenburg, Berlin, 1824/25.
King Frederick William III had a mansion built in Charlottenburg Castle's grounds using Neapolitan architecture as a reference. The king preferred not to reside in the Baroque castles of his ancestors.

could prove his extraordinary talent in his drawings that were shown at the academy exhibition. In the years of the foreign rule from France, Schinkel was influenced by German Romanticism. He was passionately interested in Gothic architecture, which was regarded as the German style at that time. He prepared architectural designs and paintings of medieval buildings. Schinkel's wish was to create a new German style based on the Gothic style with detail alterations or "improvements," the aim of which was to unite national identity and patriotic attitude.

Schinkel's first architectural works after Napoleon's defeat in 1813 all shared a certain "monument" character. Apart from their practical function, the New Guardhouse (Neue Wache) and Castle Bridge (Schlossbrücke), for example, were designed to commemorate the victory of Prussia. After Schinkel had won the king's confidence with these buildings, he was later practically overwhelmed with commissions for designs and construction plans as well as administrative tasks.

Under Wilhelm von Humboldt's influence, Schinkel's style increasingly oriented itself towards Greek culture and architecture from 1815 onwards. Along these lines, Schinkel rebuilt the Humboldt family's country seat in Tegel between 1820 and 1824 with various references to the classical Greek style. Even if Schinkel later designed numerous neo-Gothic buildings—such as Friedrichswerder Church or Kamenz Castle —, his main current interest belonged to ancient architecture. Schinkel developed from a romantic to a classical architect who left his mark on the new city of Berlin, which had at that time become known as Athens on the Spree. Programmatically, he expressed his enthusiasm for classical architecture in his great painting, "Glimpse of Greece's Golden Age", from 1825.

Although Schinkel preferred to draw on classical Greek examples in his current projects, he preserved his romantic mind and overflowing imagination that did not accept any financial restriction. Schinkel's desire for great architectural endeavours manifested itself in 1834 in the impracticable design for a royal palace on the site of the Acropolis. Schinkel's artistic outlook was therefore not aimed at purely rational and economic architecture from the start, although it is often represented in such a way. Rather, it was the king who attached importance to state building project design that would be solid on the one hand, and as inexpensive as possible on the other. Schinkel also showed special talent in this respect, however—particularly when it came to redesigning existing buildings on a relatively tight budget. His reconstruction projects never made an impression of being a temporary arrangement, either. For example, the National Theatre (Schauspielhaus) and Charlottenhof Castle give no hint at the fact that Schinkel had to include much of the old structure in his planning.

One of Schinkel's major works was the New Museum opened in Berlin in 1830 (and referred to as the "Old Museum" from the mid-19th century onwards). For him, the representative outer construction and entrance were to serve as an overture to the rationally presented art in the exhibition area. The museum building had special importance for Schinkel since its claim was to develop a sense of style in the people visiting it. As was the case with his stage sets and panoramas, enjoyment of fine art should also be an edifying experience.

Obviously, Schinkel could only carry out a small number of projects completely without outside influence. Inadequate financing, clients' wishes and consideration of existing structure to be preserved marked his working day. The reconstruction of the Academy of Architecture was one such exception—and an important one at that. Schinkel was given free rein in his capacity as both client and building authority official. This building, which was completed in 1835, allowed him to give unimpeded expression to his special interest in both functional and aesthetic architecture. Industrial buildings had provided Schinkel with new ideas on his visit to England in 1826. The Academy of Architecture was a radically modern building in its time. It is this building that made Schinkel appear as a founding father of modern architecture. But other designs by the Berlin architect also seemed surprisingly trend-setting, such as a public department store (Kaufhaus) project for Berlin's Unter den Linden boulevard.

Although Schinkel never taught at the Academy of Architecture—despite his professor's title—, one can definitely refer to a "Schinkel School." He left his mark on German architecture of the 19th century and beyond like no architect since. Schinkel could always be trusted to publicise his work and his views on architecture. As early as 1804, he pursued a plan to bring about a public reappraisal of Italian and French medieval architecture, which had been underestimated up to then, by illustrations and accompanying texts. This book project failed; however, it formed the basis for extensive studies towards an architectural textbook he worked on until his death, but never completed. The textbook was to summarise his artistic and technical knowledge and make it accessible to young architects in training. In addition, Schinkel published his drawings and completed projects in an annotated collection of designs from 1819 onwards as "Collection of Architectural Designs" ("Sammlung Architektonischer Entwürfe"). His clear outline drawings still convey an impression of how Schinkel most certainly wanted his buildings to be seen and understood at the time. The textbook and the design collection are the artistic heritage left by the architect. Not only Schinkel's build-

Two wall decorations, undated.
Schinkel not only took charge of the furnishings in his buildings, but also of the details of interior decoration, such as room textiles and wallpapers.

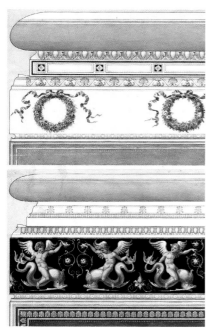

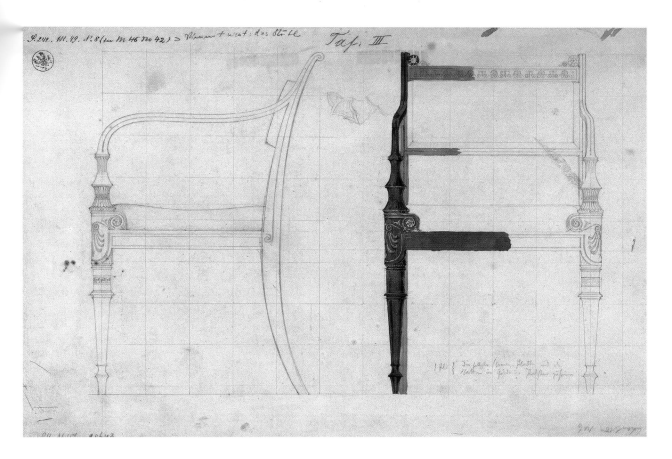

Armchair for Princess Marie's living room, Karl Friedrich Schinkel (design), Ludwig Lode (drawing), 1827.
Schinkel also designed numerous pieces of furniture. He consulted highly specialised workmen on detail drawings and execution.

ing projects, but also his paintings, drawings, furniture, interior fittings and stage sets include some of the best examples of 19th-century art. Few other artists have experienced that aura of genius which surrounded Schinkel already in his lifetime. The first biographies and appreciations of this outstanding artistic personality were written before his death. But his charisma was not limited to his lifetime; his influence has continued up to the present, ensuring his special position in the history of the arts in Germany and beyond.

1800 › Pomona Temple
Pfingstberg, Potsdam

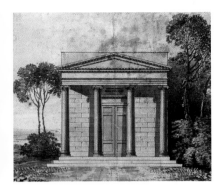

Pomona Temple design, 1800.

Wine was produced in Potsdam into the 20th century, as was the case in the rest of Brandenburg. Sanssouci, Frederick the Great's famous summer residence in the park of the same name, rises over a terraced vineyard. Vines were planted on Pfingstberg (Pentecost Hill), known as "Judenberg" (Jews' Hill) up until 1817, and in the gardens on "Heiliger See" (Sacred Lake). Since the height of the mountain offered a generous view of the surroundings, a small folly was erected there named "Temple de Pomon" after Pomona, the Roman goddess of tree fruit. From 1777 onwards, the wine terrace belonged to Samuel Gerlach, the headmaster of the city of Potsdam's school. In 1787, he bequeathed his property to his daughter, who was married to court counsellor Karl Ludwig Oesfeld.

Oesfeld made plans to beautify the terraced vineyard in 1800. The old folly, which had become derelict, was to be dismantled, and the "Pomona Temple" to be placed at a somewhat higher point. Schinkel, only 19 years old at the time, was commissioned to draw up the design of the pavilion, while its execution was carried out by a local architect. In May 1801, the building was completed. It is regarded as Schinkel's first designed and completed building—after Gilly's death, Schinkel had completed the projects that Gilly had started, but he had not been able to implement any of his own designs.

The drawing by Schinkel that has survived to this day documents the design of the small temple. The side of the building facing the terrace is decorated by a portico with four Ionic columns, and, some slight changes in detail notwithstanding, the Pomona Temple was actually completed in this fashion. Apart from a square interior, the building was characterised by a terrace placed on top of the flat roof which could be reached via a set of stairs built at the rear of the building. Protected by a sun shelter, visitors were able enjoy a broad view of the hills, rivers, and lakes in the surroundings.

View of the Pomona Temple, part of an image on a vase, Royal Porcelain Manufactory 1837/40.
The visitor was able to enjoy a marvellous view from the Pomona Temple. A sun awning protected the visitor from the midday heat.

Opposite page:
View after reconstruction.
Damaged in the war and then left to deteriorate, the Pomona Temple was reconstructed on Pfingstberg hill in 1996.

1805 · Luther Monument

Preliminary drawing, 1817.
Schinkel no longer settled for small-scale architecture in the second design phase. Rather, he designed a spacious building with a statue wall decorated with a number of figures. For his contemporaries, this called Michelangelo's works to mind.

Opposite page:
Draft design for the competition contribution for a Monument to Martin Luther, 1805.
Schinkel's design for a Monument to Martin Luther was never realised. However, the hall with vaulted ceiling was built in the Congress Memorial (Kongressdenkmal) in Aix-la-Chapelle between 1839 and 1844, albeit in another context.

Schinkel originated from a Protestant vicarage, but one can only speculate on any meaning that religion may have had for him personally. He was not an avid churchgoer, however, his work repeatedly purveys to strong religious undertones. He participated in a competition for the creation of a monument to Martin Luther on his return to Berlin from his journey to Italy in 1805. The client was a civic association from the Mansfeld district, Luther's native home. Due to Schinkel's family background the subject must have interested him beforehand. The competition also offered a good opportunity for Schinkel to return to the public arena after his journey abroad.

Various professors at the Berlin academy participated in the competition; among them were Heinrich Gentz, one of Schinkel's former teachers, and Johann Gottfried Schadow, the sculptor. Schinkel designed a single-vaulted hall with a semicircular arch and open steps. The design had a classical feeling with its pillars, capitals (column heads) with figures and acroteria (construction elements at the apex of a structure), while the interior widened to a rib-vaulted apse. Architectural forms from the classical and Gothic styles were merged into one design. The hall provided room for a statue of Luther. Gnarled German oaks framed Schinkel's monument drawing, symbolising Luther's steadfast "Teutonic" character. However, the building itself would hardly have actually paid tribute to Luther, in whose honour the monument was to be built. Only a few years later, Schinkel would already master this art in an accomplished manner with his Mausoleum for Queen Louise. In 1806, however, Schinkel's design was not taken into consideration; but Schadow, who had designed a monumental statue, was awarded the commission.

The French occupation of Prussia interrupted all plans for the Mansfeld monument in 1806. In 1815, King Frederick William III, the patron of the monument project, completely took over all planning work. He summoned Schinkel, Schadow and Rabe, a building inspector, to a commission that was to provide new designs. As was the case in the Memorial Cathedral to the Wars of Liberation, Schinkel included plenty of sculptural decoration in his architectural design. Schinkel's contemporaries compared his design with Michelangelo's ingenious work for Pope Julius II. The king was also impressed by the amazing talent of his "appointed architect," but also expressed the opinion that Schinkel had to be "reined in." It would have cost a fortune to implement his design, which, for that reason, did not stand a chance of being realised. Instead, Schadow was awarded the project, and his statue was officially inaugurated in Wittenberg's market square in 1821. Schinkel was only left with the design contract for the cast-iron canopy.

1810 ‣ Mausoleum for Queen Louise
Charlottenburg castle grounds, Berlin

Design for the Mausoleum for Queen Louise, façade, 1810.

The king wanted the mausoleum of his deceased wife to be situated at the end of a dark pine avenue. In contrast, the ornate, almost cheerful tomb seems to shine outwards from the inside.

In 1810, Queen Louise died unexpectedly at the age of 34. Her death was deeply mourned by her subjects. She had become a figure of hope through her courageous attempt to lessen the consequences of war after Prussia's defeat at a personal meeting with Napoleon. King Frederick William III ordered a Doric temple to be erected as a mausoleum to the queen; the mausoleum was built in the Charlottenburg castle grounds (Charlottenburger Schlosspark) at the end of a pine avenue. Schinkel was involved in drafting Heinrich Gentz's design work.

Soon after construction started, Schinkel introduced his own counter-design to Gentz's mausoleum at the academy exhibition. As there was no possibility of its being implemented, he designed an ideal building—a neo-Gothic chapel façade projecting from thick tree vegetation. Raised on steps, the arched hall with pointed vaults is surrounded by exquisite decorations. Four delicate angels are floating over slender pillar groups; the hall opens out to flowery designs that have hardly anything in common with the Gothic style. Despite its purpose as a mausoleum, Schinkel's design appears somehow cheerful. The mausoleum seems to shine from the inside. Slender pillars carry a rib-vaulted roof that makes the interior appear like a palm grove. The place of the altar is taken up by the grave itself, surrounded by three angels. The apparently sleeping queen is represented as a holy martyr. Schinkel described the intended effect thus: "The light falls through the windows from three niches that surround the resting place from three sides; red twilight shades gently pass through glass panes of rose-red colour, spreading over the entire architecture that is fashioned in white marble."

Unlike the classical mausoleum that was actually built, Schinkel's design was friendly, inviting. It was intended "to give a cheerful view of death, which only the true religion, genuine Christianity, grants to those devoted to it." Correspondingly, he developed a Christian Gothic chapel that was quite unlike a classical heathen temple. Apart from that, Schinkel did not intend his mausoleum building to be a private memorial. Rather, it was intended for public access: "One should have a sense of well-being in this hall; it should be open to all people, to lift their spirits in its comfort." Louise's monument was meant to be a sign of hope for the burgeoning national feeling and, at the same time, should symbolise the rebirth of the state after the devastating defeat at the hands of Napoleon.

Schinkel also considered Gothic to be a patriotic style. However, he did not strive to copy any existing building. Construction and stylistic effect give the building a new impact with freely invented, individual forms. Schinkel was searching for a new German national style in which tradition and artistic invention were to be given equal emphasis. Although his visionary mausoleum design was not actually realised, he was still commissioned to complete the Queen Louise Monument in the Gransee market square in 1811.

Opposite page:
Design for the Mausoleum for Queen Louise, interior, 1810.

1813 · Gothic Cathedral by the Water
Painting

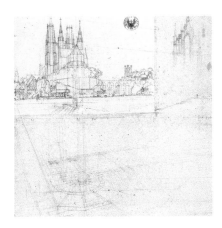

Study belonging to the painting "Gothic Cathedral by the Water", 1813.
To represent the (fictitious) cathedral correctly, Schinkel designed a detailed ground plan on which to base the painted church building.

Opposite page:
Gothic Cathedral by the Water, copy by Wilhelm Ahlborn from the 1813 original by Karl Friedrich Schinkel, 1823.

Schinkel may have been a self-taught painter, but some of his many paintings were commissioned by high-ranking personalities. Their charm lies in their precise execution and romantic atmosphere. He mostly painted architecture set in romantic landscapes, with the people he painted stimulating the scene, but also carrying the atmosphere of the work.

Among other things, Schinkel was inspired by the sketches and drawings he had made on his travels. But his joy in the invention and reconstruction of historical or fantasy buildings also shows through his paintings. Most were completed before 1815, when he only had a few architectural tasks to complete. During this time, a period in which he painted medieval cathedrals is particularly noteworthy. "Gothic Cathedral by the Water", created in 1813, is one of Schinkel's most significant paintings. While the original work is lost, an excellent copy has been preserved.

The painting illustrates a medieval town located by a river at sunset, with people working on the near side of the quay. On the opposite shore, a monumental series of steps leads up to the cathedral, which towers above everything else. The town, partly in sunlight and partly in the shade, spreads out on either side. Churches, merchant houses, a great viaduct and even a small ancient temple on the bank of the river stand witness to the town's history and prosperity. However, the centre of attention is still the cathedral as it majestically rises against the evening sky, obscuring the setting sun in such a way as to appear partly as a silhouette, and partly illuminated by the setting sun.

The cathedral in Schinkel's painting is not a copy of any existing building. Schinkel had closely studied medieval cathedrals on his travels, but for this painting, he designed a new architectural wonder for which he had made precise design drawings beforehand. It was not Schinkel's intention to show merely an existing town. By placing the church above everything else in the painting, he created an architectural and social utopia. For Schinkel, the Gothic style also had political overtones—the hope of a new, strengthened society nurtured by Germany's past to carry prominent civilian traits is shown in this picture. In his rediscovery of "old German art", Schinkel was in harmony with the emotional world of the Romantic period. Caspar David Friedrich, who created a similar atmosphere in his paintings, was one particular role model for Schinkel.

Mappe XX N° 248. Tab. 105.

1814 · Memorial to the Wars of Liberation
Design for Leipziger Platz ▸ Berlin

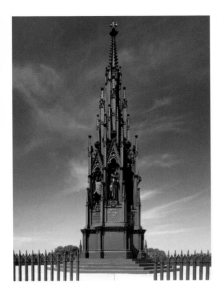

Kreuzberg Monument, Berlin, 1818–21.
The Kreuzberg Monument resulted from Schinkel's plans for a memorial cathedral. Made of cast iron, it was set up on the highest point before the gates of Berlin. Angels personify the battles of the wars of liberation. The Iron Cross medal designed by Schinkel crowns the monument.

Opposite page:
Design for Memorial Cathedral to the Wars of Liberation, 1815.
For the Memorial Cathedral in Leipziger Platz, Schinkel adopted not only the planned installation site but also the monumental base of Gilly's monument to Frederick the Great. This podium was not typical of Gothic buildings.

The victory over Napoleon ended foreign rule in Germany in 1813, and triggered a wave of patriotism. It was the aim of Prussian middle-class society to unite the scattered German principalities into one nation-state. This endeavour is also mirrored in the planning of national monuments such as the Leipzig Battle of the Nations Monument, or in the desire to complete Cologne Cathedral.

King Frederick William III also planned a victory monument—not at a place of significance for the whole nation, but at the centre of his realm, Berlin. On the strength of his paintings of medieval cathedrals, Schinkel was commissioned to design a Gothic memorial cathedral in 1814. Schinkel's project went far beyond a simple architectural design since this cathedral was to unite varying claims and expectations. It was to provide room for services and patriotic victory commemorations. As a sculpture, the cathedral was to reflect the victory over Napoleon, and also to represent the entire history of the nation. Its primary purpose was to arouse feelings of purification in the visitors to the cathedral through its artistic essence, and provide moral strength to society. All artistic and financial energies of the state should be united in completing this building project. Schinkel was hoping for improved training for artists and artisans as a side-effect.

Schinkel's architectural design consisted of three elements: the massive tower that projects upwards towards a filigree spire, the nave, and a large-sized dome construction. A massive podium—hardly conceivable in the traditional Gothic style—would lift the building from its urban surroundings, underlining its purpose as a monument. Schinkel adopted the podium and the site (the planned location was Leipziger Platz) from Friedrich Gilly's design for King Frederick's monument. The message that the building was to purvey manifested itself in the dome, particularly in its outer construction. Monuments to the Prussian rulers depicted on horseback and statues of Prussia's "historical and latter-day heroes and statesmen" were to be built on the load-bearing buttresses of the vaulted ceiling. Sculptures in the upper dome area would symbolise the divine order and at the same time manifestly legitimise the monarchy. Coats of arms and the Iron Cross on the spire were to create a reference to Prussia.

Schinkel planned to build statues of theologians, scholars and artists—representatives of the civil sphere, at the pillars in the interior of the nave. The podium was to take the remains of the nation's heroes, thus augmenting the "holiness of the location."

Schinkel's memorial cathedral was never built, most probably due to its enormous cost. However, a reflection of its planning can be seen in the Kreuzberg monument inaugurated in 1823. Schinkel's cathedral concept was put into effect here, albeit in reduced form; only the uppermost part of the spire rises into the Berlin sky.

1815–1818 · New Guardhouse

Neue Wache ▸ Unter den Linden 4, Berlin

Opposite page:

Historical photograph by Waldemar Tintzenthaler, 1902.

The changing of the guard always attracted numerous onlookers. The guards had to stand in front of the building and greet passing members of the royal family. The building was flanked by monuments of famous generals.

The planning and construction of the New Guardhouse between the years 1815 and 1818 represented the turning point in Schinkel's career. After the early buildings before his travels in Italy, the New Guardhouse was the first great construction project that Schinkel was able to realise. King Frederick William III still inhabited the Crown Prince's Palace after his accession to the throne since the uncomfortable Baroque castle of his ancestors did not hold any appeal for him. Opposite his residence, between the armoury and the university, was an artillery guardhouse that had become an ugly sight over time. Just to increase the value of the surroundings of his residence, the king ordered a new building that would also contain guard posts and sleeping quarters for the soldiers of his First Regiment.

At first, Schinkel intended to erect the Guardhouse at the end of the existing chestnut grove. Italian loggias from the Renaissance served as the basis for the planned hall with semicircular arches; the location at the end of an avenue resembled the design for the Mausoleum for Queen Louise. Like the queen's monument, the Guardhouse was also to serve as a national memorial—as a monument to the wars of liberation.

But Frederick William III declined Schinkel's first design and required that the Guardhouse be moved forward to the front of the street, if only to be able to view the new building from his residence. Schinkel had to experiment with various designs before he could reconcile the role of a monument with that of a building with an actual use.

According to Schinkel himself, the design was to be based on that of a Roman Castrum, a military base; the four corners of the building are formed like towers. The main front is adorned with a Doric column portico with pediment. An ancient battle scene in the tympanum was to reflect the Prussian victory; the scene was not sculpted into the tympanum until after Schinkel's death. Small goddesses of victory designed by Johann Gottfried Schadow were set into the entablature between the columns and

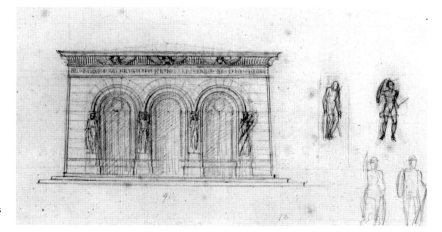

Design drawing for the New Guardhouse as a hall with vaulted ceiling, 1815.

Schinkel made numerous studies for the guards' building on Unter den Linden. He set great store by both the architectural effect and the use of monumental sculptures. This sheet shows various sketches related to the project.

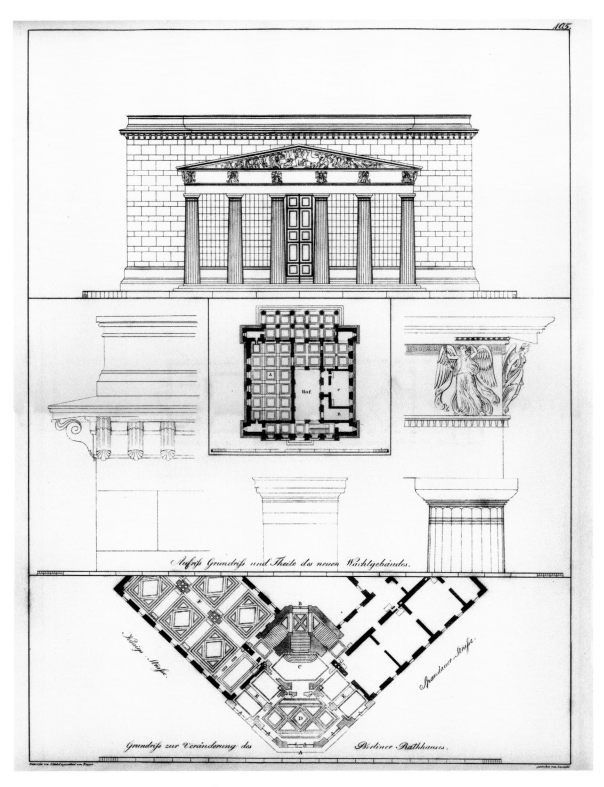

Aufriß Grundriß und Theile des neuen Wachtgebäudes.

Grundriß zur Veränderung des   Berliner Rathhauses.

Front elevation.
The corner risalites projecting from the New Guardhouse were designed to be reminiscent of a Roman Castrum.

pediment, replacing the triglyphs characteristic of Doric temples. Despite the general likeness to classical forms, Schinkel deliberately diverged from the usual classical architectural style in combining Roman and Greek architectural elements in his Guardhouse design. The inside of the Guardhouse was arranged for simplicity. The building's two-storey interior contradicted the monumental outer building, as did the asymmetrical ground plan.

Statues of famous generals from the wars of liberation were erected in front of the Guardhouse and on the opposite side of the street. Furthermore, Schinkel planned to expand Berlin's Unter den Linden boulevard into a "via triumphalis" lined with statues on either side. However, all that remained of this plan were the sculptures on Castle Bridge.

With the New Guardhouse, completed in 1818, Schinkel had established himself as an architect. With his architectural design, he skilfully achieved a monumental effect in this relatively small building. The king subsequently entrusted him with the most important construction tasks of the Prussian capital within the following decades.

Opposite page:
New Guardhouse; elevations, ground plan and architectural details.

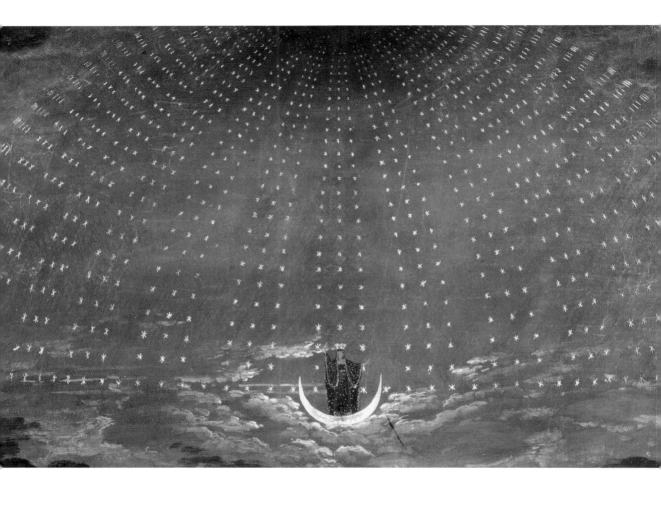

1816 ‣ Stage Sets for the "Magic Flute"
Royal Opera House ‣ Unter den Linden, Berlin

Left-hand side:

Stage set design for the "Magic Flute" opera, "Palace of the Queen of the Night," act I, scene 4; 1815 .

The starry dome of the Queen of the Night probably is Schinkel's best-known stage set. The Queen herself appears stationary on a crescent moon. Schinkel found his inspiration for this in medieval representations of the Madonna.

Water-colour by Eduard Gärtner, around 1832.

Mozart's "Magic Flute" was performed for the first time in 1816 at the Royal Opera House, which was built by Georg Wenceslaus von Knobelsdorff between 1741 and 1744; the stage sets were designed by Schinkel.

Schinkel was already enthusiastic about theatre as a child, and had designed his first stage sets in 1798. However, he did not work on theatre projects until 1815. By then, he had his long-standing experiences with his "visual perspective illustrations" to call back on, where illusionistically painted backgrounds, skilful illumination and moving figures had given the observer the impression of viewing a real landscape. Schinkel transferred these design principles to his theatre stage sets, thus revolutionising stage design.

The Baroque theatre had tried to portray space as broad as possible by cunningly layered scenery and illusions of perspective. But the perspective only seemed right when viewed from the king's box; most spectators had to put up with a restricted view and annoying distortions. Schinkel's stage construction was fundamentally simpler. It consisted of a background that was easily interchangeable and painted on canvas with an unchanged front stage. Light and colour only symbolically hinted at the space and atmosphere of the action. Superficial illusionistic deception was avoided, as was the case in classical theatre. The result was an improved view from any position. Schinkel's stage sets were also cheaper and quicker to change.

But Schinkel's stage designs were not only technically innovative; they created a brilliantly effective synthesis of visual and architectural characteristics. His immense historical knowledge of architecture and style was included in the designs. Apart from their visual attraction, his stage sets developed a certain popular-arts appeal. Schinkel was immensely successful with his designs—he designed at least 126 backdrops for 50 stage plays. Opera performances modelled on Schinkel's stage set design are shown to this day.

Schinkel's most famous designs were those that accompanied Mozart's opera, "The Magic Flute". This was also his most extensive stage-decoration contract with its 12 stage sets. The premiere took place in the Unter den Linden Royal Opera House (Königliche Oper) on January 18, 1816, on the festive occasion of Frederick I's coronation anniversary as the first King of Prussia on January 18, 1701. The effort was enormous—not only in the gigantic painted stage sets; the grid also had to be raised to allow the backdrops to be pulled up to their full extent. The performances became a great popular success with much acclaim. Not only Schinkel's architectural visions but also their scenic essence and the strong lighting effects enthralled the audience. The best-known backdrop was used for the appearance of the Queen of the Night. She appears standing on the crescent moon with the stars of the firmament arranged into a dome. Other scenes put more emphasis on Schinkel's architectural interest—architectural visions that also purveyed a strong atmosphere arose in a blend of fantasy and archaeological reconstruction.

**Stage set design for the "Magic Flute,"
"Sarastro's Garden", sphinx in the moonlight,
act II, scenes 7-12; 1815..**
Influenced by Masonic thought, Mozart's opera
was set in Egyptian culture. Schinkel represented
ancient Egyptian forms in his "Sarastro's Garden"
and other decorations. Buildings such as the
sphinx and the pyramids led the spectator to the
fascinating, exotic country on the Nile.

Karl Friedrich Schinkel: Stage set design for the "Magic Flute", "In front of the mausoleum," act II, scene 7; 1815.
In addition to the painted decorations, lighting effects played a decisive role in Schinkel's stage sets. Night scenes or the rising sun aroused utmost astonishment from the spectators.

1818 – 1821 ▸ National Theatre

Schauspielhaus ▸ Gendarmenmarkt, Berlin

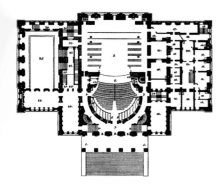

Ground plan of the first upper floor.
The entrances as well as the foyers and cloakrooms were located in the podium of the building. The theatre hall itself with the semicircular auditorium, a two-storey concert hall and side rooms were situated on the upper floor.

Opposite page:
Front view.
With its temple front and the monumental outdoor staircase, Schinkel's National Theatre dominates Gendarmenmarkt still today. After being reconstructed from the damage it sustained in the war, the building no longer serves as a theatre but as a concert hall.

The national theatre built by Carl Gotthard Langhans (the architect of the Brandenburg Gate) stood in Berlin Gendarmenmarkt since 1801. The long building was located between the symmetrical dome churches of the German and French parishes, set somewhat to the back. The theatre looked fairly plain in its architectural surroundings; the Berliners made fun of its design for its roof, which was shaped like a "suitcase" or "coffin."

When the theatre burnt down to its foundations in 1817, many architects applied for its reconstruction, but Schinkel won acceptance for this prestigious reconstruction project. Not only were his designs convincing; his concept combined practicality, beauty and fire protection in the most economic solution possible. The new theatre was to become a "work of art accomplished in every aspect, completely harmonising on the outside and inside." This was not an easy bill to fill, especially since it was not a new building. Columns and masonry that had been spared by the fire had to be reused to economise on costs. The king also required additional storerooms, restaurant facilities, a concert and banquet hall, and a rehearsal stage in the new theatre.

Schinkel knew how to include royal wishes into his design skilfully—even if this meant reducing the size of the auditorium. He turned the hall previously positioned across the building by 90 degrees. In the space that was freed within the foundation walls to the side, he was able to accommodate a two-storey hall to the north and the additional rooms required to the south. This resulted in three parts of the building, whose solid dividing walls reduced the danger of fire.

Both the theatre and stage had to be significantly reduced in size within the existing walls; the stage itself was only 12 metres wide. Schinkel tried to combine a good view and good acoustics for the largest audience possible in the auditorium. The three balconies were carried by iron columns so as not to obstruct the view where feasible. Smooth surfaces were avoided. The small size of the room and sculptural decorations were intended to improve acoustics.

The banquet hall in the southern side was decorated with Ionic columns and ornamental sculptures to create a "cheerful character," in the words of Schinkel. The painted ceiling, the busts of composers as well as decorative details indicated the function of the room as a concert hall.

In the outer construction, the auditorium and stage shared a common roof, thus projecting out of the rest of the building, which was layered like a pyramid. The ground floor and podium of the building lifted the theatre above the ordinary level of town architecture as if it were on a pedestal. A great set of open stairs led to the theatre's column portico built in front of the auditorium. Since the building was to be entered via the podium of the building, the open stairs had no function other than to give the theatre an air of dignity as a temple of art. And this is exactly how Schinkel wanted the building to be regarded. The tympanum depicts Apollo in a chariot drawn by griffons. The sculptures, reliefs and architectural forms emphasise the origins of theatre in ancient Greece.

Schinkel promoted the architectural motif of the tomb of Trasyllos, the ancient Greek choir master, as the basic design concept in his theatre wall design—a design not otherwise common in classical architecture, a façade articulated by pilasters. The outer walls did not seem to consist of walls with window apertures. Instead, they appeared dissolved into the load-bearing supports and heavy entablature. Only the columns of the portico, which Schinkel had to preserve, formed an exception.

The National Theatre was destroyed during the Second World War. The building was not reopened as a concert hall until 1984. While the outer construction was largely rebuilt according to the original, the auditorium was not reconstructed—an over-enlarged copy of the small Schinkel concert hall took its place. Today's National Theatre conveys Schinkel's architectural ideas only in its outer construction.

Design drawing for the auditorium of the Berlin National Theatre, 1818.
Schinkel's plans for the auditorium were largely realised when the building was reconstructed. The ornamentation was altered later. The compact dimensions of the room and the sculptural decorations were designed to ensure good acoustics.

Two-storey concert hall (destroyed in 1945).
Based on the comparatively small hall of Schinkel's original National Theatre, a substantially larger central concert hall was reconstructed.

1821 – 1824 · Schlossbrücke
Unter den Linden, Berlin

Detail of the iron parapet, designed in 1819, cast in 1824.
The railings designed by Schinkel are decorated with sculptures of water creatures. He thus expressed the function of this bridge spanning the Kupfergraben in a most decorative fashion.

Opposite page:
View of the Cathedral and the Old Museum from across the bridge.
The 33 metre wide Castle Bridge spans the castle moat, the Kupfergraben, with three arches. With the aid of a tilting mechanism, in former times ships could pass without problems. This unusual feat of engineering and the enormous building costs involved made the bridge one of the most important construction projects in Schinkel's Berlin.

"This Dogs' Bridge (Hundebrücke), as they call it, near the most beautiful buildings of the residence devalues this area so much that a change which corresponds to the surroundings must be carried out." Thus was King Frederick William III's verdict in his letter to Schinkel in March 1819. It contained the request to replace the old wooden bridge that led to the castle in continuation of Berlin's Unter den Linden boulevard. It had long since been referred to as the dogs' bridge because of the hunting pack accompanying the Elector to the Tiergarten (zoological garden). It was first named Castle Bridge when the foundation stone was laid in 1822. Schinkel himself had already made the suggestion of replacing the narrow bridge by a new, appropriate structure in connection with the building of the New Guardhouse. This suggestion was part of Schinkel's overall plan to redesign the grounds around Berlin Castle.

In 1819, he presented his plan for a solid stone bridge, which was to span the Kupfergraben moat in full street width at almost 33 metres. One particular problem in the building of this splendid bridge lay in the fact that it would have to be designed as a drawbridge to let shipping vessels pass. On the published drawing, Schinkel did not, however, include the technical details for the movement of the bridge. Schinkel left to posterity an ideal presentation of his Castle Bridge, which was one of his most significant enterprises in Berlin in his lifetime, if only due to the immense cost of almost 400,000 German Talers.

But the technical challenge and high costs alone do not constitute the significance of this bridge. Having in mind eight sculpture groups, Schinkel planned to raise the building from its practical function to the status of a monument. He designed one nude warrior accompanied by a goddess of victory for each sculpture group. Like the New Guardhouse, Schinkel intended to design the bridge as a memorial to the heroic deeds of the wars of liberation only a few years before. When the foundation stone was laid, he announced that the sculptures "were to give our youngest descendants a marvellous memory of the fight for freedom and independence, which the king and its people have so gloriously won."

While the bridge—completed in 1824—was being built, the king cancelled the sculptures so elementary to purveying the significance of this architectural structure from the project. Whether this was due to cost alone or also due to the exaggerated bourgeois monument character the statues would have evoked, can only be speculated on today. Only after the death of his father in 1840 did Frederick William IV—a great admirer of Schinkel—have the sculptures realised. The skilfully formed cast-iron gratings with tritons, sea-horses and dolphins were the only decorations included on the bridge in Schinkel's lifetime. These, as Schinkel explained, were to "remain as a reminder for those crossing the bridge that they are above the water," despite the width of the street.

1820 – 1824 · Tegel Castle

Schloss Tegel ▸ Adelheidallee 19 – 21, Berlin

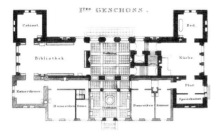

Ground floor plan.
The vestibule, recognisable by the floor covering, is located in the centre of the country manor. The old structure that had to be included into Schinkel's development plans is drawn in a lighter shade; the new construction is darker.

View into the vestibule.
When rebuilding the residence, Schinkel created a state reception room on the ground floor. Two Doric columns subdivide the hall decorated with works of art. The ancient St Calixtus fountain is situated in the centre.

Opposite page:
View of the park side façade.
Compact and radiantly white, Tegel Castle with its four towers is embedded in a spacious landscaped park. Features of Italian villas are interwoven with Greek forms and classical-style architectural sculptures.

Schinkel had already become acquainted with Wilhelm von Humboldt, who had been a Prussian diplomat at the Vatican at that time, in 1803. Humboldt and his wife Caroline had kept up their friendship with Schinkel. Humboldt's intercession had significantly led to Schinkel's employment in the civil service in 1810. Schinkel received the commission to rebuild Humboldt's country house in Tegel in 1820; Tegel Castle, as it was known, was to become the married couple's country seat.

The manor house, located amidst charming scenery, dated from the 16th century and, before its reconstruction, was a long, two-storey building with a tower. The rather inconspicuous old building was to be given a stately appearance, particularly since it was also to be opened to the public—Humboldt's collection of antiques that he had purchased in Rome was to be exhibited there. The distinctive humanistic ideals of the head of the household and his preference for Greek art and culture were the deciding factors in Schinkel's planning of the new home.

Schinkel had already given a glowing demonstration of his talent in redesigning old buildings in the National Theatre project. He also created an astonishing result in Tegel. He doubled the base of the country house while reusing the existing walls. Integrating the existing tower, four three-storey extensions were built at the corners. The building also received a third, gallery-like upper floor. When the building was completed in 1824, it was not only reminiscent of the grace of Italian villas through its radiant white colour, but also included individual motifs from Greek antiquity. The reliefs on the towers were copied from the Tower of the Winds in Athens. On the one hand, the reorganisation reminded the owners of their happy Italian years. At the same time "the architectural ideal of an intellectual life of education" arose, as Andreas Haus put it in his book, Karl Friedrich Schinkel als Künstler (Karl Friedrich Schinkel as an artist). This becomes evident in the architectural type—more villa than castle—as well as in the outer wall articulation. As was the case in the National Theatre built at the same time, Schinkel modelled the arrangement of the pilasters in Tegel on the ancient Trasyllos

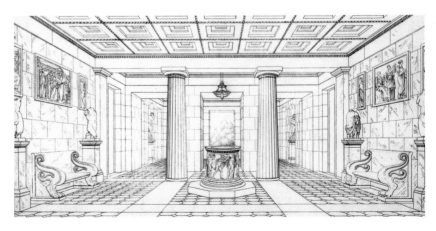

monument. Tegel Castle was therefore also built for the edification of its visitors, even if it was only partly open to the public.

The inside design, which has remained almost unchanged to this day, also answered this claim. The important collection of antiques was placed for presentation in the entrance hall and in the hall of the upper floor. Schinkel replaced the original, solid wall on the ground floor with two Doric columns. In the centre of this state room stood the most important exhibit, the ancient Calixtus fountain, for which the pope had personally issued the export permit. Ancient sculptures and reliefs were arranged on Ashlar-style walls. As he did later in the Berlin Museum project, Schinkel consciously positioned ancient works of art next to free-standing columns. Plaster casts of ancient sculptures were exhibited on the upper floor. Rotating pedestals made it possible to study the sculptures from all sides and under changing light directions. Modern methods of museum design were thus used in Humboldt's country house, anticipating their later implementation in the Berlin Museum. At the same time, this architecture designed by Schinkel, with its art collection, furnishings and landscaped park, created the feeling of an inhabitable work of art. Today the building and surrounding premises are privately owned. Public access is therefore restricted to certain areas and special occasions.

Antiquity hall on the upper floor, photo from around 1935.
Wilhelm von Humboldt's collection of sculptures was given special emphasis in the building. The most important ancient sculptures were concentrated in the antiquity hall as precious plaster casts.

Wilhelm von Humboldt in his study, anonymous painting from around 1830.
Humboldt also surrounded himself with ancient works of art in his study. To him, they embodied the artistic and social ideals of Greek culture.

Wilhelm von Humboldt's Tegel Castle study, photograph from 1910.
This historical photograph shows the room with its original furnishings. In the background, one can see the scholar's famous library, which disappeared without trace after the Second World War, as did the furnishings.

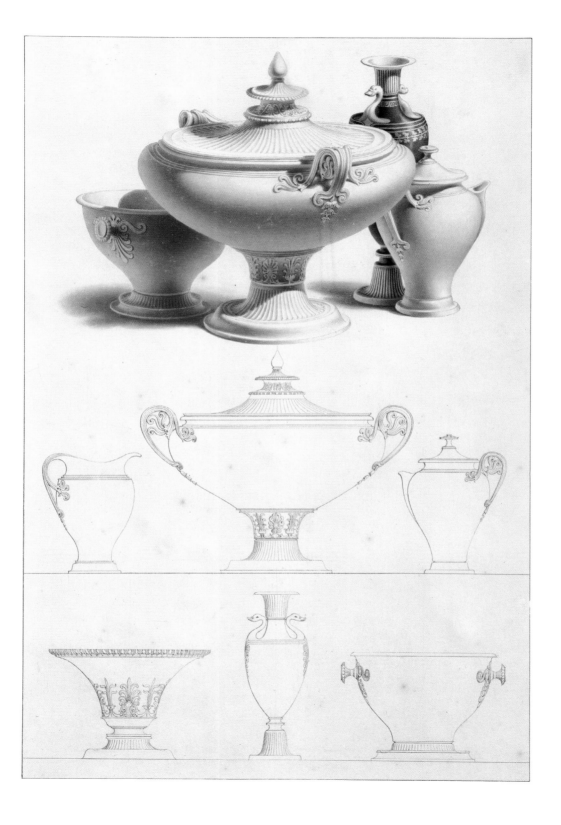

Textile designs, 1821.
In the third section of the examples collection, Schinkel and Beuth included exemplary textile designs which bear a fascinating wealth of colour and decoration.

Opposite page:
Design drawing for vessels, 1821
The illustrations and design drawings clearly show the ceramics designed by Schinkel. They were to be used by Prussian craftsmen as models for their own works.

At the beginning of the 19th century, the situation of the Prussian skilled crafts was destitute. Besides the lack of orders after the defeat against France, the main reason was that there had long since been no modern, comprehensive training. Most apprentices were still being introduced to their profession in technically backward family-owned enterprises, and the trades simply missed out on the technological progress of industrial nations striving for progress such as England. Local production therefore had little chance of measuring up against the foreign competition as far as quality and design were concerned. There were also serious export setbacks. The Prussian government reacted to this situation by attempting to introduce sweeping reforms in the trades and skilled crafts.

Before 1800, the Royal Academy of the Arts had already occasionally made attempts at improving production conditions, e.g. at the Royal Porcelain Factory. Between 1804 and 1806, compulsory guild membership was finally abolished to encourage the formation of new private companies. One reform intention was also to impart sound scientific and technical knowledge to craftsmen.

To bring about this transfer of technology, the Royal Technical Committee for Trade ("Königlich-Technische Deputation für Gewerbe") was founded in 1810. The eight employees in this committee were affiliated to the Prussian trade ministry. Peter Christian Beuth, a friend of Schinkel's, was appointed its director in 1819.

Matching the example of the General School of Architecture (Allgemeine Bauschule) founded in 1799, the Technical Committee introduced plans for the first higher "Technical Trade School" (Technische Gewerbeschule) for skilled craftsmen in Berlin in 1821. Besides a laboratory and workshops, the school also had a collection of designs and models as well as a library with an associated design section at its disposal; many new ideas and concepts were conveyed to a new generation of craftsmen in this institute. The aim was to enable both craftsmen and merchants to produce marketable products again. In order to provide them with suggestions in aesthetics in addition to technical matters, Beuth and Schinkel published the design collection "Examples for Manufacturers and Craftsmen" from 1821 onwards. The large-size, carefully designed drawings were delivered one by one, and the two editors collaborated on writing an accompanying text to each design. Under the aegis of the state, the sheets were distributed to libraries, draftsmen's schools, the appropriate authorities, and artists free of charge; they were never commercially traded. The publication work was not completed until 1837. Beuth self-confidently wrote in the preface that "work executed in this way will always remain classical and never cease to fulfil a useful purpose."

The "Vorbilder" were subdivided into three sections: 1. Architectural and other forms of decoration; 2. Devices, vessels and smaller monuments; 3. Examples of textile decoration. The individual examples covered a broad range of products, materials, techniques and forms. Vessels of all different types, building sculptures, weaving patterns, metalwork for fences, woodwork for parquet floors, glass work, chandeliers and decorative weapons could be produced and realised using these designs. The examples recommended were copies of works of art from Classical Antiquity and the Renaissance on the one hand, and on the other, Schinkel – the only contemporary artist – even contributed his own designs in which he also orientated himself towards the classical style. It was his intention to combine the principles and the ethos of the ideal (classical) form with the latest in materials and production techniques.

However, one should not misinterpret the intentions of the two editors. It was certainly not their aim to elevate craftsmen to the level of independent artists. On the contrary, Beuth warned the craftsmen "not to fall to the temptation of designing the work themselves, but diligently, faithfully and tastefully imitate the work done before them."

Schinkel gained influence in arts-and-crafts production particularly in the field of iron casting. Unlike many other branches, Prussian metal casting, known abroad as "fer de Berlin," was certainly highly developed. Schinkel valued the advantages that cast iron offered – high stability, low material costs and the possibility of serial production – in his own architectural designs as well as his commercial arts-and-crafts products. He designed iron furnishings for the royal gardens in Berlin and Potsdam from 1820 onwards, some of which are still produced today.

Cast-iron table, Royal Iron Foundry in Berlin, designed around 1830.
Numerous items of cast iron furniture were made in Berlin, an important centre for cast iron manufacturing. The design for this table is ascribed to Schinkel.

Opposite page:
Ancient tripods from Herculaneum, engraving by Johann Mathäus Mauch, 1821.
Illustrations of classical arts and crafts that were frequently copied in the 19th century were also included in the examples collection in addition to Schinkel's designs. Schinkel also referred to these examples in his work.

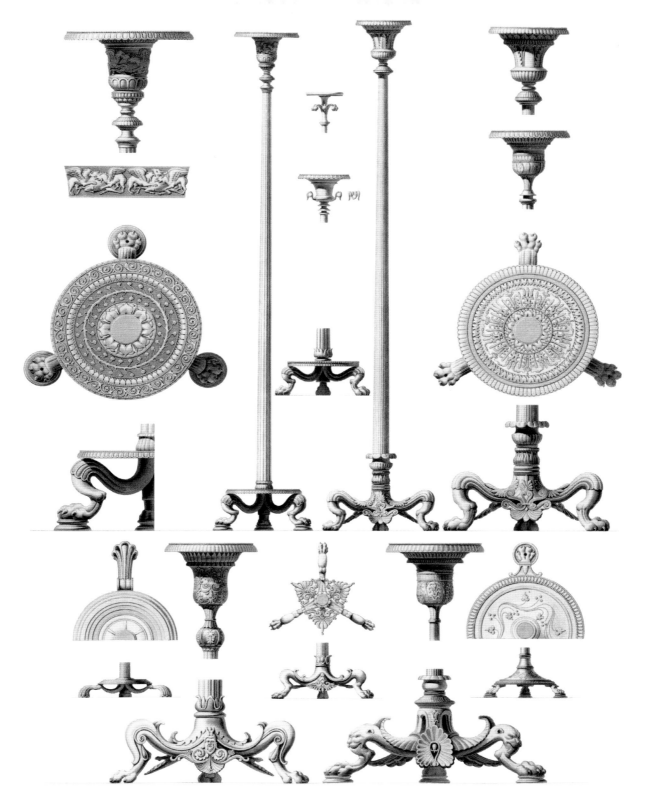

1823–1830 · Altes Museum
Lustgarten, Berlin

Opposite page:
View into the rotunda of the Old Museum.
Schinkel modelled the central room of the museum on the ancient Pantheon in Rome. Particularly valuable classical sculptures were placed between the columns.

View from the Lustgarten (Pleasure Garden).
The monumental main facade of the museum is dominated by 18 Ionic columns. A cubic construction conceals the dome of the rotunda.

The idea of setting up a museum in Berlin arose in 1797. Works of art hitherto hidden in castles were to become "a school of education in taste" in a museum accessible to the public. Schinkel prepared his first designs for a museum in 1800. However, the planning only took definite form after 1815. Napoleon had carried the most important European works of art off to Paris. After his defeat, Berlin's art treasures also returned to the city. There was an increasingly vociferous desire for public exhibition of the returned art that had been taken as the spoils of war.

After archaeologist Alois Hirt had finally presented a museum design and drawings for a new building, Schinkel also presented his design. He surpassed Hirt's architectural design by far. The king entrusted Schinkel with the construction in 1823. As a location, he planned the museum to be built in the pleasure garden located opposite the castle. It had become a sad sight, having been used as a parade ground since the beginning of the 18th century. Schinkel recognised the significance of this location in urban development. He noted: "The beauty of the area will be completed through this construction [of the museum] by filling the fourth side of this beautiful old square in a dignified manner." Berlin's centre of representation was to be enlarged splendidly with this new building.

The old museum, as it has been called since the middle of the 19th century, was an impressive sight with its façade's broad design. 18 Ionic columns were set up close together in a line on high pedestals between two corner pillars. The monumental façade was designed to be overwhelming in its simplicity. Only the window apertures and the continuous cornice on the other three outer walls provided a hint at the two-storey interior. At the front entrance of the building a visitor would ascend a broad set of open stairs leading up to the narrow columned hall. Behind a second row of columns, a double set of stairs led to a generous landing, which provided a view of the pleasure garden up to Friedrichswerder Church. The boundary between indoors and outdoors became blurred; the museum was a public space. These stairs were one of Schinkel's most ingenious room creations, turning a museum visit into a ceremonial event.

The museum was arranged around two inner courtyards. Its centre consisted of a large rotunda which Schinkel modelled on the Roman Pantheon. The dome not only served as a reception area and foyer leading into the different areas of the collection. "Here, the sight of a beautiful and noble room must create an atmosphere of pleasure and the recognition of what this building holds," as Schinkel noted. Twenty Ionic columns supported the continuous gallery. Ancient statues were erected between the columns, making the hall a magnificent introduction to the museum collection. Daylight passed through an oculus in the glorious coffered dome as it had done in its Roman equivalent. Rich forms and coloured materials endowed the room with a noble atmosphere. Getting the visitor in the right mood was of such major importance to Schinkel that he devoted approximately a third of the total area of the building to the rotunda and staircase in his plans.

Ancient and modern sculptures were erected on the ground floor of the museum. The floor was subdivided into smaller units by columns. Partitioning walls were used on the upper floor to create smaller cabinets in which paintings were hung close together, arranged by schools of painting. The exhibition rooms were not laid out for representation purposes, in contrast to the rotunda. They served as serious places of

View of the Lustgarten (Pleasure Garden) as seen from the upper landing of the staircase, watercolour painting by Michael Carl Gregorovius, 1843.
The museum's staircase represents one of Schinkel's most impressive construction designs. The boundaries between the inside and the outside become blurred. The two rows of columns and the raised vantage point of the observer create an interesting view.

View beyond the Kupfergraben, 1823.
On the right-hand side, the old cathedral reconstructed by Schinkel can be recognised. Alongside the Castle and the Museum, it served as an architectural enclosure of the Pleasure Garden.

study. The museum was opened on August 3rd, 1830, on the 60th birthday of Frederick William III, and was Europe's most modern museum building in its time.

Originally, an extensive fresco series illustrating topics "from the educational history of mankind"—as Schinkel noted in a memorandum of 1823—was also part of the architect's museum design. These paintings were already mentioned in his earliest designs. Between 1828 and 1834, Schinkel prepared six detailed drawings showing the development of mankind and its virtues with various motifs from ancient mythology. But like the sculptures of Castle Bridge, the fresco series was not realised until after Schinkel's death. The frescos designed by Schinkel were carried out until 1855 under the management of Peter Cornelius; further illustrations in the Schinkel style were later painted onto the other walls. The frescos were to fulfil the purpose of arranging the cultural heritage of mankind in a greater context of intellectual history that was set out in the museum's exhibits. The wall paintings were largely destroyed during the Second World War; they were not replaced when the building was reconstructed. Only a few fragments survived. The interior layout was also altered after 1945.

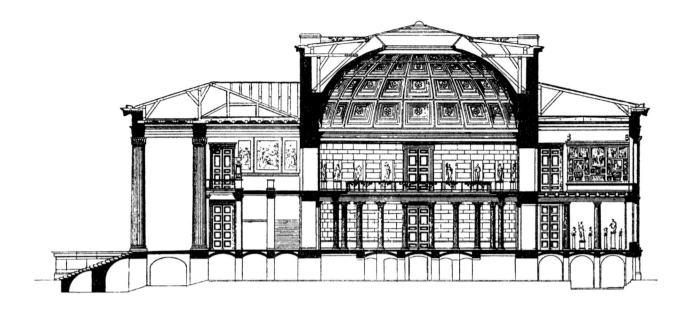

Above:

Cross-section of the building.
The rotunda and the magnificent staircase with Schinkel's wall paintings (on the left) take up a considerable portion of the total area of the museum. Paintings and sculptures are exhibited in the wings surrounding the inner courtyards.

Right:

Ground plans of the ground and upper floors.
The two main floors of the museum are laid out for the presentation of paintings and sculptures. The pictures were presented in small cabinets on the second upper floor. One floor below, the sculptures were exhibited in a room layout subdivided simply by columns.

Opposite page:

View into the colonnade, photograph from 1915.
The monumentality of the columned hall underlines the significance that Schinkel attached to art. In this view, Schinkel's wall paintings still can still be recognised. Severely damaged during the Second World War, they were removed later.

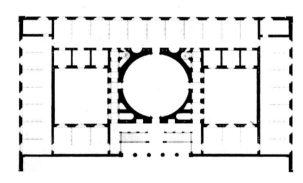

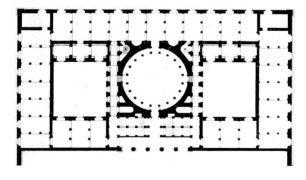

1824–1828 · The Crown Prince's Apartment

Berlin Castle ▸ Schlossplatz, Berlin

Crown Prince Frederick William IV (from 1840, King Frederick William IV) in his study and living quarters in Berlin Castle, around 1846, painting by Franz Krüger.
Crown Prince Frederick William IV designed his own living quarters in Berlin Castle with Schinkel's help. Important medieval and Baroque rooms particularly remained untouched; other rooms were arranged in a classical manner.

Crown Prince Frederick William had lived in the rooms of Frederick the Great's former residence in Berlin Castle since 1816. The heir to the throne did not receive approval to alter the Rococo-style rooms until 1824, after his wedding. His designs served as Karl Friedrich Schinkel and his employees' specification for furniture and room layout; the work lasted until 1828. Even if only three rooms could finally be equipped according to the original plans, the Crown Prince's apartment was decorated according to one of the most excellent interior designs of that time.

The crown prince and his wife had six main rooms and several utility rooms in the north-eastern side of the castle. The oldest part of the building still preserved, the late-Gothic St Erasmus chapel used as living accommodation since the middle of the 18th century, was also part of the living quarters. The crown prince set up his homely, medieval workroom under the late-Gothic vaulted ceiling that had once again been laid open. Numerous collection cabinets, drawing archives, paintings and sculptures corresponding to his artistic interests were to be found there there. Schinkel planned the room's equipment according to the original construction. The seating he designed had Gothic forms, but the furnishing remained neutral in style. The architect's careful handling of the historical rooms can also be seen in Frederick II's former office furnishings, which remained unchanged in their delicate, but then outmoded Rococo style. Elizabeth, the Princess Royal, used the rotund room as an office.

The connected former concert room of the great royal predecessors remained as a function room. Even so, it was completely rearranged. Like at Charlottenhof, which was being reconstructed at the same time, an exedra, in this case a semicircular divan, took up a special position. The bench at Charlottenhof provided a border to the raised terrace; here, the exedra was part of the indoor furnishings. However, the awning painted on the ceiling and the room's green plants gave one the impression of sitting under an open sky. The walls of this inviting room were elaborately arranged. A panel of narrow wall cupboards went all around the room, serving as the base for figure consoles with sculptures protruding into a frieze of panoramas. Both sculptures and paintings showed figures from the ancient world of gods and mythology. Like Humboldt's country seat, this room was reminiscent of the classical Greek period. But family tradition was also considered in Berlin Castle, as individual rooms also paid tribute to the late-Gothic period, the peak of the elector's powers, and the time of Frederick the Great.

Nothing has remained of the drawing-room apart from some Tieck sculptures. The Crown Prince's apartment designed by Schinkel perished in the middle of the 20th century, together with Berlin Castle.

Opposite page:
Tea room, view to the west, around 1830; anonymous watercolour painting.
The awning painted on the ceiling and the green plants behind the circular seat lend the room the impression of being outdoors.

Above:

The Erasmus Chapel in Berlin Castle, 1839, watercolour by Johann Heinrich Hintze.
The old Erasmus Chapel in Berlin Castle was made usable for living purposes by installing a drop ceiling.

Left:

View of the castle from the southeast, painting by Maximilian Roch, 1834.
The crown prince and his wife's living quarters were located in the south-eastern corner of Berlin Castle on the 2nd upper floor. The old Erasmus Chapel projects from the façade at the wing on the Spree side. The tea room is located in the castle wing on the street side.

Opposite page:
View into Berlin Castle's tea room.

View into the interior.
In his drawings, Schinkel knew how to present his buildings to the best effect. Skilful perspective drawings with human figures dramatise the buildings.

Opposite page:
View of the main façade.
Originally, Friedrichswerder Church was part of a narrow urban development context – residential buildings, later also the building of the Academy of Architecture, surrounded Werderscher Markt. The place of worship is still there today, but on its own, largely without any surrounding buildings.

Friedrichswerder Church owes its name to Friedrichswerder, a Berlin district not far from the Royal Castle, where mainly workmen and refugees of faith had been settled after the Thirty Years' War. A riding house converted in 1700 served the German and French parishes as a place of worship. Since 1819, the king had been considering rebuilding the church, which had become dilapidated. Schinkel examined the designs submitted as the construction official responsible. Dissatisfied with these, he submitted counterproposals of his own. He referred to examples from the classical period, having turned away from his earlier romantic, medieval architectural ideals. But the king and the crown prince required the church's reconstruction in the Gothic style. Complying with the order, Schinkel also developed designs for a neo-Gothic place of worship. In 1824, he presented four projects to the king for his decision. The preserved plans show two neo-classical and two neo-Gothic churches. The neo-classical plans differed only in the choice of style, not in the basic design; one is kept in the Doric style, while constitutes an example of the Corinthian order. In both cases, a cylindrical dome construction that was to accommodate the choir was built onto the neo-classical temple with columns. On the other hand, the neo-Gothic designs varied in the façade. As an alternative to the solid one-tower church, Schinkel suggested a design with two more delicate corner towers. He supplied two corresponding alternatives for the interior—a Gothic hall with pilasters and a stellar vault or a classical Roman interior. The construction system and floor plans in the two designs are similar, but the room's effect is amazingly different. Every part of the building is transformed from one style into the other with virtuosity.

The king decided in favour of Schinkel's Gothic two-tower church design in 1824. The church was completed by 1830. The new church was built with a brick façade to match the new material aesthetic. According to his preference for classical architecture, Schinkel chose for Friedrichswerder Church a Gothic style that was as plain as possible. A "neo-classical Gothic style" was the result of going back to construction principles of the classical period—the clearly structured forms of the church only remotely draw on the medieval Gothic brickwork style; they have nothing in common with Gothic wall construction. Buttresses only just projecting out of the surrounding structure and the strong horizontal wall structure are more reminiscent of the static design of the classical period. The gable roof typical of medieval churches is missing; a parapet hides the flat roof. Schinkel did not use the Gothic pointed spires, but cubic towers inspired by the English Decorated style. The delicate interior of the church contrasts with the stark outer construction. The coloured building materials and the paintwork together with the upward striving architectural style form a harmonious whole.

1825 · Glimpse of Greece's Golden Age
Painting

Schinkel's painting, "Glimpse of Greece's Golden Age", was created as a wedding present from the city of Berlin to Princess Louise in 1825 on her marriage to Dutch Prince Frederick. Unlike the "Medieval Cathedral on the Water" painted in 1813, this picture is dedicated to Greek culture, which had by now dispelled Schinkel's earlier preference for medieval art. Through Wilhelm von Humboldt, the owner of Tegel Castle, Schinkel had already recognised an ideal that was not only artistic but also had a social context in the classical Greek period. According to Humboldt, "The Greeks conceived an education of the whole person; they are to us what their gods were to them."

The elongated rectangular painting had a size of 94 x 233 cm. The image composition and subject of the painting set Schinkel's work significantly apart from the way that classical Greek buildings were represented at that time. The usual representations showed overgrown ruins in a generally melancholic style depicting the fall of the giant empire. As the title implies, Schinkel illustrated ancient Greece as a blossoming culture. The construction of a new temple dominates the complete foreground in the image. Only the topmost part of the building can be seen. The observer, who might face a light attack of vertigo, is, as it were, situated on the scaffolding. The figures in the picture guide the eye of the beholder into the event portrayed in the painting. Artists and workmen are busy finishing the building—part of the entablature richly decorated with sculptures is just being positioned. The eye wanders outward towards the hilly landscape. On the left, a group of soldiers approaches the temple. Several impressive monuments and mausoleums are located on the hill in front. A prospering town with palaces, temples and public buildings stretches through the valley. The planned settlement tells much of Schinkel's urban development ideals.

The painting has no connotations of idealistic nostalgia. In this archetypal work, the painter rather propounds his view of the present and future, the restoration of a culture worthy of admiration. With his buildings in Berlin, which was often called Athens on the Spree, Schinkel wanted to create the impression of an ancient ideal which was also socially relevant in his own time. His vision for a future society also expresses itself in this painting: "One can live in the picture with this [distinguished] people and pursue the same in all matters, political or purely human."

But it is also the painter's intention to bring nature and cultivated activity of man into harmony. Schinkel once said about his paintings: "The attraction of the landscape is increased by drawing specific attention to the traces of human influence, either through a people enjoying their earliest golden age ... or through a landscape that mirrors the wealth of a highly educated culture that knew how to use that aspect of nature skilfully to create increased enjoyment of life in general for its people."

1826 – 1829 · Charlottenhof Castle
Potsdam

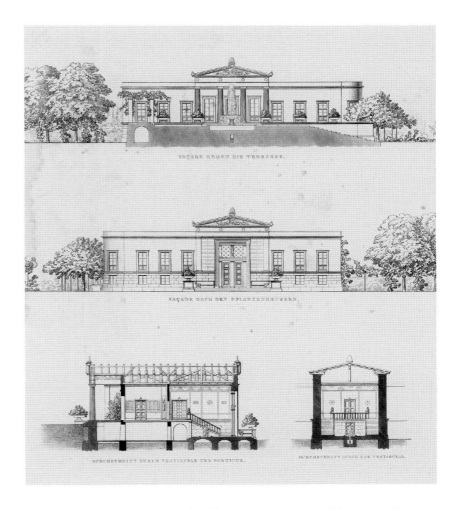

Views and cross-sections.

The king purchased an estate south of the Sanssouci park, which he gave to the crown prince as a Christmas gift in 1825. Like his brothers, Frederick William was also to receive a summer residence in Potsdam. Karl Friedrich Schinkel took charge of the project's planning. An 18th-century manor house was located in the spacious area. Plans by landscape gardener Lenné integrating the property into the castle grounds were enclosed in the gift title documents. The artistically inclined crown prince was particularly enthusiastic about architecture. He had already enjoyed Schinkel's tuition in design and architecture. The Charlottenhof reconstruction project was therefore jointly planned by the client and the architect; Lenné was consulted for the park design.

The existing building was not very large. It consisted of a podium and a main floor as well as a steep roof. The plan was to change the country house into a villa in the clas-

sical style—it was to serve as a retreat for the prince, and also pay tribute to his admiration for the classical style. As usual, Schinkel had to use as much existing structure as possible for cost reasons. The basic structure, window apertures and inside walls remained almost unchanged. Nevertheless, the building was changed beyond recognition when the reconstruction work was completed. The steep roof was removed, and a raised temple roof placed over the middle of the main body of the house. A semicircular bay window in the crown prince's master bedroom gave the couple a panoramic view of the park. After the alterations were completed, Charlottenhof took the appearance of a neo-classical villa of simple elegance.

The park's ingenious design also made a great contribution to the new effect. Soil was deposited on the garden side completely covering the podium of the house. An exedra, a semicircular bench, was positioned at the end of the terrace so as to permit a view of the villa, the park and Frederick the Great's new palace. Viewed from the garden side, Charlottenhof appears as if it had only later been installed into a classical temple. Fountains, vine-covered pergolas, sculptures and water troughs enhance the Mediterranean charm of the complete estate.

The castle had ten rooms on the main floor, some of which were rather small in size. The state rooms—a vestibule, a drawing-room and a terrace—were located along the central axis of the building. These led on to the private rooms on the northern side of the building. The interior décor, which is still extant and was partly designed by Schinkel, is particularly noteworthy. The guests' area was situated to the south of the drawing-room. The most original room was the "tent room" (Zeltzimmer), which took the effect of a camping tent with its blue-and-white striped lengths of fabric. The ser-

Opposite page:
View into the hall with the red doors.
The garden hall is the real state room of the small castle, situated on the middle axis of the building. It lies behind the column portico of the garden front.

vants' quarters were located on the podium floor. Charlottenhof already gave the impression of a middle-class summer residence due to its small size. The castle was only planned as a provisional arrangement, though. Schinkel and the crown prince planned a spacious group of buildings to the west of the area. The villa in the Toscana that had been described by Pliny, the classical author, was to be rebuilt here. However, like so many of Schinkel's designs, this great expansion of Charlottenhof remained unrealised.

From 1829 onwards, the "Roman Baths" ("Römische Bäder") were built near the castle. The main purpose of the baths was to create a pleasant place to stay. The asymmetrically arranged buildings were grouped around several inner courtyards and opened up to alcoves and pergolas. The main building was the only building to have a practical use, serving as the gardener's residence.

The crown prince again took part in designing this picturesque complex. Schinkel probably also had some influence on the planning, which was mainly entrusted to Ludwig Persius, an architect and Schinkel pupil. Examples of rural Italian architecture that Schinkel had become acquainted with in 1804 on his Italian travels were incorporated

Pink Room.
Schinkel referred to classical examples for the wall design and the furnishings. The painting frieze – modelled on the Pompeian painting style – shows female figures.

Opposite page:
Tent Room.
The guests of the crown prince and his wife stayed in this room, which was set out like a tent. Alexander von Humboldt, the explorer and world traveller, also frequently stayed here.

Roman Baths in Sanssouci Park, four caryatids in front of the bathing niche.
Copies of the caryatids in the Erechteion on the Acropolis in Athens decorate the bathing niche. The interior rooms, decorated with paintings and sculptures, provide a surprise for the visitor, who hardly expects classical architectural elements inside these buildings with their rural external appearance.

Opposite page:
Roman Baths, 1829–39, view of the entrance area.
The Roman baths buildings, clearly based on rural architecture in Italy, include a gardener's flat. Most of the other rooms were not lived in. The crown prince only used the Roman baths for short stays.

into the Roman Baths. At that time, he had been planning to write a publication on these largely unknown medieval buildings. In the Roman Baths at Charlottenhof, various architectural styles form a collection of buildings which seem to have grown over a considerable period of time. Schinkel characterised it as "a grouped whole like a painting that would present diverse pleasant views, secret resting places, cosy rooms and open spaces offering the pleasure of country life."

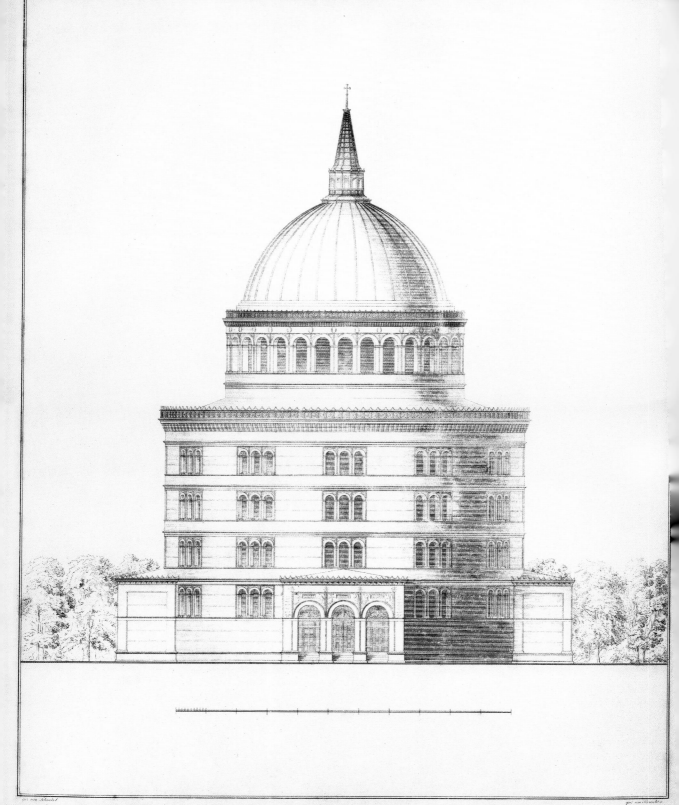

ANSICHT DER KIRCHE IN DER ORANIENBURGER VORSTADT BEI BERLIN. NACH DEM ENTWURF N° IV.

1828 – 1835 · Suburb Churches

Berlin experienced a rapid population increase in the first third of the 19th century. New residential areas grew for the less well-off strata of society, particularly to the north of the old city centre. In February 1828, Frederick William III assigned Schinkel the task of building two new churches to ensure pastoral support in Oranienburg, a suburb of Berlin. With 2,500 to 3,000 seats each, they almost doubled the size of the cathedral or Friedrichswerder Church. The special attraction of this task for the architect lay in being able to design outside the town centre "Protestant churches meeting only their inner purpose". Schinkel need not take any possible neighbouring buildings into consideration.

Schinkel presented five designs in August 1828. The "church as a perfect circle" and the "church with vestibule" provide good examples of the depth of variation in Schinkel's architectural designs. The cylindrical church was one of the architect's most radical designs. He broke completely with the conventional appearance of Gothic or Baroque churches—the four-storey place of worship looked more like an industrial building than a church. The only reference to the church's purpose was the drum dome with lantern.

On the other hand, Schinkel's design of a church with a vestibule, strongly orientated towards classical architecture, was far more traditional. However, the rectangular ground plan with the staircases located in corner rooms was also designed for high functionality. The king selected two designs with rectangular ground plans.

As Schinkel himself emphasised, the building costs were disproportionately high compared to the number of seats in these enormous churches; economically, building smaller churches would make more sense. The large building plans were therefore withdrawn on his initiative. However, his designs remained as a planning basis, although he reduced them in scale in 1829.

After finishing the first planning phase, construction work was not started until several years later. On the one hand, the king and crown prince had different opinions on church construction. On the other, a cholera epidemic had also struck Berlin, which prevented swift construction. When in 1832 attention could finally be turned towards the completion of the churches (construction work of the church later named St Elizabeth's had already started), the social situation in the northern suburbs had deteriorated due to the epidemic by such a degree that the king now requested the erection of four churches. This was to ensure improved pastoral care in the population and prevent possible public unrest.

St Elizabeth's was already under construction, but was modified to be larger than the other three churches and had two galleries when it was finished. The three other churches (St Paul's, St John's, and the Church of Nazareth) followed the simple scheme of a rectangular church building with a gently sloping roof and only one gallery. The tower, vestibule and other architectural features were abandoned. The grounds and the building cost estimates were the same for all three new buildings. Since Schinkel, however, did not want to build identical sacred buildings, he tried to give each

Opposite page:

Design for a church as a perfect circle, 1828. For the northern Berlin suburbs, Schinkel presented five different designs for large churches that were to offer space to as many visitors as possible, and also be realised at a reasonable price. The circular ground plan and the simple wall design constitute a break with tradition in sacred architecture.

church an individual design. Two of the churches were brick-built and had round arches, while the two others were based on classical designs with plaster walling. The construction work on the four suburban churches was completed in 1835. Regrettably, not one of the churches' interiors has remained unchanged to this day. Even worse, St Elizabeth's is still a ruin after its destruction in the Second World War.

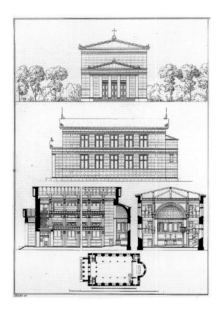
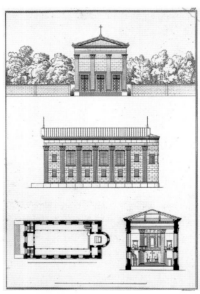
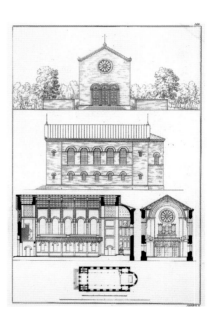

From left to right:
Elevation, cross-section and ground plans of St Elizabeth's, St Paul's, St John's and the Church of Nazareth.

Left:
St Elizabeth's, Berlin-Mitte, 1832–35
(ruin since 1945).

Right:
St Elizabeth's, Berlin-Mitte, view into the
chancel (destroyed).

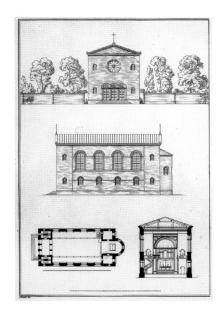

Church of Nazareth, Berlin-Wedding, 1832–35.
The outer structure of the Church of Nazareth has
largely remained unchanged, and represents an
example of Schinkel's simple but monumental
design. For cost reasons, the architect had to
refrain from including a bell tower in the church.

1832 – 1835 · Academy of Architecture
Bauakademie ▸ Werderscher Markt, Berlin

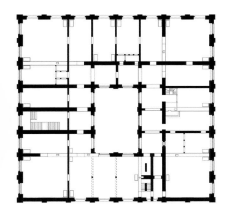

Ground plan of the 2nd upper floor.

Opposite page:
The Academy of Architecture in Berlin, 1868, painting by Eduard Gärtner.
The Academy of Architecture appeared as a radiantly red cube in its urban surroundings. The large private accommodation of the architect was located in the 2nd upper floor of the building, together with his studio and office; this is shown by the curtains in the painting. After Schinkel's death, the first Schinkel Museum was set up here. Friedrichswerder Church rises up behind the Academy of Architecture.

The last building in the centre of Berlin that Schinkel designed was the Academy of Architecture, completed between 1832 and 1836. It was probably his most important and most radical work. The building was pulled down in 1960 although it had largely survived the Second World War intact. Endeavours to reconstruct the museum led to a corner of the building being rebuilt on a trial basis in recent years. The building was located in close proximity to Schinkel's Friedrichswerder Church with only the Kupfergraben moat separating it from the Baroque Hohenzollern Castle.

Schinkel had been a pupil of the "General School of Architecture" himself. At the height of his architectural career, he was to design new buildings in these state facilities which were to house further institutions. Shops on the ground floor served to provide additional financing for the project. The first floor was kept for the Academy of Architecture itself. The second floor was to house the building authority (Oberbaudeputation) as well as Schinkel's atelier and working residence. The topmost mezzanine was limited in its usefulness due to the roof sloping towards the inner courtyard.

The Academy of Architecture was a four-storey building on a square ground plan. Each of the four sides measuring 46 metres in width and 22 metres in height was designed to be more or less identical to the others. The building's reflection in the Kupfergraben moat appeared as a cube. The exterior building consisted of eight uniform window axes each, whose regularity gave no indication of the inner floor plan or use. Pilasters emerged from between the window axes and through the cornice forming projecting stone parapets. They lent a vertical continuity to the façade, which was augmented by the pattern of the brickwork in part glazed violet. However, horizontal ledges restored the façade's balance. There was no central emphasis in the façade; there were even two main entrances.

The door and window frames were richly decorated with industrially produced terracotta tiles. The decorations drew attention to the purpose and educational nature of the Academy of Architecture. Portraits of famous architects were put up at the entrances, and the ancient architectural style inventions were allegorically represented. A programmatic cycle was shown under the windows of the upper floors, representing the decline of old architecture and the rising of a new architectural form. Schinkel had striven all his life for this architectural renewal.

Schinkel's journey to England in 1826 had given him an important impression that affected the design of the Academy of Architecture. In the English Midlands, he had enthusiastically visited industrial buildings built without decoration or classical architectural layout. The emphasis there had been on function and construction, while decoration and architectural style played a subordinate role. Under this influence, Schinkel set himself the challenge of designing a public building in the middle of Berlin that promoted building materials and construction as the dominant expression of architectural design. This most probably resulted from the fact that, functioning as both client and construction official, he was largely free to draw up a design as he pleased. He based his planning on a grid. Brick-built pillars serving as supports for the

Left:
Window with terracotta sculpture, photographed around 1910.

Centre:
The staircase, photographed between 1907 and 1911.

Right:
View into the rebuilt air well, photographed between 1907 and 1911.

vaulted ceilings were erected at the intersection points of the individual 5.5 x 5.5 metre grid segments. Load-bearing walls were unnecessary in this building. The different floors could be individually partitioned according to the needs of the various occupantsof that floor. In some aspects of the basic layout, Schinkel anticipated what would later become the rule in the frame construction of modern multi-storey buildings. In the Academy of Architecture project, Schinkel put his technical and artistic ideas to the greatest effect. As Schinkel's pupil Friedrich Adler noted, this was understandably the architect's favourite building. According to the judgement of Schinkel's biographer, Waagen, architecture's ideals were exchanged with its essence in the Academy of Architecture.

Schinkel's Academy of Architecture was also a link to the future. Of course, it was still a long way from the functional aesthetics of architecture's modern era in the 20th century. However, architects such as Ludwig Mies van der Rohe and Peter Behrens could well regard themselves as Schinkel's heirs, regarding the Academy of Architecture.

The Academy of Architecture under construction; section of the town panorama painted from the roof of Friedrichswerder Church, painting by Eduard Gärtner.

Gärtner's photographically exact city panorama directs the viewer's eyes to the then completed shell of the Academy of Architecture building. A corner of Berlin Castle is visible on the left behind the building site.

The Academy of Architecture, photographed around 1888.

The Academy of Architecture was recognised soon as one of Schinkel's major works. A monument, standing there again today, was set up to the architect on the square in front of the building.

Vault of the dance hall.
The two-storey dance hall is crowned by a stellar rib-vault.

Opposite page:
Babelsberg Castle seen from the River Havel, view and ground plan.
Only the first stage of construction up to the massive octagonal tower, which houses the dance hall, was realised from Schinkel's plans for Babelsberg Castle. The southern wing (on the right) was later completed by Schinkel's successors in altered form.

Babelsberg Castle is situated in the picturesque river and lake area of Potsdam's garden region. From here, Potsdam, Glienicke Castle and the New Gardens can be viewed. It is hardly surprising that landscape gardener Peter Joseph Lenné regarded this as an ideal place to build the Castle. In 1826, he drew the attention of Prince William—who was later to ascend the German throne as Emperor William I—to the location; for a summer residence in Potsdam was also to be built for him.

Prince William was married to Augusta of Saxony-Weimar, who very soon became enthralled by the Babelsberg building project. In her opinion, a neo-Gothic castle in the style of an English mansion should be built there. She had illustrations and diagrams shipped in from England to serve as a basis for designs she herself created. However, King Frederick William III was sceptical about this new and expensive building project since this would involve constructing a completely new castle, rather than renovating or extending an existing building as was the case with Charlottenhof.

It was not until the planning for the new castle had been reduced to the dimensions of a modest English cottage that the king gave his approval in 1833, after which Schinkel immediately received the commission to design this summer residence. Of course, William and Augusta did not think for a moment of making do with the approved cottage. Schinkel was far-sighted enough to design a neo-Gothic asymmetrical building to fit into the side of the hill, which was to be built in two building phases.

He arranged the buildings along a rising line that would reach its highest point at the western flag tower. This round tower with its arched windows supposedly constituted the oldest part of the building. Babelsberg Castle, according to Schinkel's approach, was to appear as a castle in the old style that had grown over time—not only through the arrangement of buildings, but also through the historically varied styles. The first building phase was carried out between 1834 and 1835. Only the eastern two-storey tract from the open pergola to the octagonal tower was erected under Schinkel's management. The new building had a base that was almost square, and there was a festival hall in the octagonal tower.

The extension that turned Babelsberg Castle into the installation which still exists today, was only carried out between 1844 and 1849, after Schinkel's death. Ludwig Persius and Heinrich Strack were responsible for the project, and carried out a more stylistically varied façade design than the one Schinkel had planned. Babelsberg remained as the preferred summer residence of William, also after his coronation as the Emperor of the German Empire in 1871.

1834 · Royal Palace on the Acropolis
Athens, Greece

Opposite page:
Interior view of the large state hall.
The large hall was to form a ceremonial centre of the residence of the Greek King Otto of Bavaria. The intricate architecture and the use of sculptures are based on the classical Greek style to from a connection between the new ruler and Greece's glorious past.

In Prussia, Schinkel's imagination was only too often checked by the need to economise. In 1834, however, his opportunity to implement one of his great designs finally seemed to arise. Bavarian Prince Otto of Wittelsbach had been elected King of Greece in 1832, and needed a residence in Athens. In Munich, the Prussian crown prince, who was married to a Bavarian princess, recommended Schinkel for the new construction of a palace on the Acropolis.

Greece was the unattained aim and model for the artists of Schinkel's era. The prospect of being able to design a residence on the Athenian castle mountain—on sacred ground—was a thrilling thought. Schinkel had plans to develop the entire mountain plateau, but without touching the highly valued ancient buildings. However, the ruins would be surrounded by buildings in the style of single-storey Pompeian villas forming groups around inner courtyards. Gardens, fountains and a hippodrome would have given this sea of debris the cheerful appearance of a classical villa settlement. The centre of the new residence was to be a large reception hall. Schinkel's design showed a high hall opening to an inner courtyard surrounded by columns; four colossal round columns would carry an elaborately constructed open roof truss. Colourful materials and rich sculpture decoration would lend a genuinely royal character to the indoor space. It is striking that Schinkel did not plan any reconstruction or extension based on the style of the ancient Acropolis; rather, he used the Roman style, not time-honoured classical Greek antiquity as a model for the new buildings. He therefore avoided intermixing the existing structures with the new buildings.

Today the mere thought of converting the "world cultural heritage" that was the Acropolis into a place of residence for a head of state would be inconceivable. In Schinkel's era, however, the idea of turning what was left of the great edifice into a usable building while preserving its ruins was undoubtedly a very tempting thought.

Ground plan.
The ground plan reveals the complex system of the new buildings planned. Schinkel intended to develop the western part of the mountain plateau from scratch. On the other hand, the entrance side of the Acropolis (on the left) was to enthral the visitor with a racetrack and parks as well as a view of the ancient ruins.

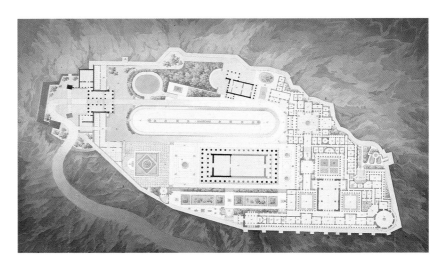

Schinkel completely overestimated the resources of the impoverished Greek state in his planning. A letter from Prince Pückler in Athens brought sobering news in March 1836. Although King Otto was fascinated by Schinkel's design, it was not feasible— "They would have to send along Phidias and Kallikrates [Greek artists of the antiquity], and above all, the material resources afforded to Pericles. We are so poor here that we are not even able to repair the road to the Pentelicon [the marble quarry]." In recognition of his efforts, Schinkel was awarded the Greek Order of the Redeemer. However, in his reply to Pückler, the dejected architect wrote that all of his "youthful fancy and beautiful illusions" had been destroyed.

View from the town.
The enormous extent of the new buildings planned is revealed in this side view. The gable of the "Large Hall" rises over the buildings that are highlighted by a colonnade on the right. On the left, the viewer can see the reconstruction of the statue of Athena Promachos that Phidias, the classical sculptor, had created around 450 BC.

Opposite page:
Cross section of the mountain plateau.
The ruins of the famous Parthenon, the largest temple of the Acropolis, would not have been affected in any way by Schinkel's development.

1838 · Orianda Castle
Yalta, Ukraine

In the same year that Schinkel started his plans for Kamenz Castle, Frederick William III's daughter, Princess Charlotte, also referred to Schinkel for a palatial building project. She had been married to the Russian Czar Nicholas I since 1817, and had adopted the name of Alexandra Feodorovna.

In 1837, the czar and his wife had travelled to the Crimea. The coastal landscape of the Black Sea in the south of the Russian empire had impressed them as much as the historical region south of the Caucasus. In the 19th century, many country residences of Russian nobles had already been built in these Mediterranean-like surroundings.

Especially Orianda, situated on the banks of the Black Sea, appealed to the czarina, so Czar Nicholas gave her the property. Filled with enthusiasm, she immediately informed her brother, Crown Prince Frederick William, that she would like to have a country retreat built there that would remind her of Charlottenhof Castle, which she had visited in 1829.

Consequently, Schinkel was commissioned to design Charlotte's Crimean residence. He was sent elevations and plans of the area to be developed since the Castle was to be harmoniously embedded into the landscape. He was not able to travel to Russia because of his many building tasks in Prussia. When the Russian royal couple visited Berlin in 1838, they discussed the planning for Orianda Castle. Once again, the crown prince also participated in the designs; he wanted his sister to have a castle that would combine rural attractiveness with the cultural significance of the location, and represent the social status of the czarina. Orianda would be worthy of the noblest imperial house on earth, as Schinkel assured his client.

As far as Schinkel was concerned, only artistic styles that were part of the intended location were suitable for the palace. After a proposal in the Old Russian style—modelled on the Kremlin in Moscow—the final design was of a palace in the classical Greek style; Crimea had been colonised by ancient Greece. Soon, the extent of the building project had nothing in common with the more modest Charlottenhof.

Like the Acropolis design, Orianda Castle was to follow on from classical Greek culture. However, there were no illustrious ruins that could be included in the palace residence. For that reason, Schinkel placed a museum at the centre of the buildings. The art collection was to be kept in the substructure of a glass-faced lookout tower in the form of a temple that towered above the other buildings to lend the palace further significance. According to the architect, this "Museum of the Crimea" was to contain works collected from all classical Greek provinces along the Caucasus to Asia Minor, so that one could take in the enjoyment of ancient art while promenading the residence. The massive pillars and unvaulted ceiling structures of the grotto-like museum were reminiscent of classical buildings that had also existed in the Crimea. In contrast to the dusky museum, Schinkel planned a bright, well-lit temple built above it. The vegetation in the building was to remind the visitor of the hanging gardens of Babylon, one of the seven wonders of the ancient world. In size and status, Orianda Palace was to match the culture of the classical period and the political power of the owner.

Opposite page:
Elevation of the narrow front of the Belvedere and cross-section of the Taurian museum, 1838.
A museum of ancient sculptures and other antiquities from the region was to be placed in the foundation of the central temple, which soared above everything else. The hanging gardens at the building were to call to mind those of Semiramis, one of the seven ancient Wonders of the World.

When the czarina finally received Schinkel's designs, the size and the architectural scale of the project disturbed her. In April 1839, she wrote to her brother, asking him why "he [Schinkel] would not design a smaller, feasible project instead of this impossible venture that should earn Mithridates' successor fame, but provide little joy in living, and would not be finished before we have grown old." It is therefore little wonder that Orianda Castle, like the palace on the Acropolis in Athens, was never built.

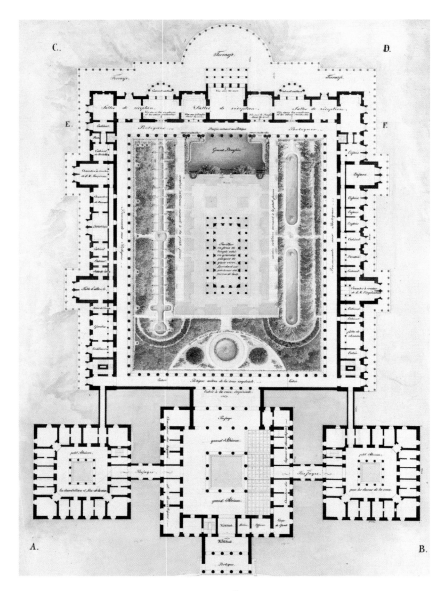

Ground plan, 1845.
The visitor was to reach the gigantic, garden-landscaped inner courtyard through one of the three square entrance buildings; the building was to open to the sea with a terrace and columned halls (above).

Elevation of the façade facing the sea and the entrance wing with the three atria, cross-section through the royal court, 1838.
The temple and vantage point, glazed and embedded in luxuriant vegetation, was to rise above the main body of the castle to provide a view of the romantic, beautiful landscapes on the Black Sea.

Elevation de la façade C.D. du plan.

Elevation de la façade A.B. du plan.

Coupe selon E.F. du plan.

1838–1873 · Kamenz Castle
Kamieniec Zabkowicki, Poland

Main view (so-called valley side).

Opposite page:
View into the inner courtyard, 2000.
With its merlons and well-fortified round towers, Kamenz Castle creates a military impression. Open pointed-arch arcades surround the large inner courtyard.

Ground floor plan intended for realising Kamenz Castle, with court hall and outbuildings, 1838 (war loss).
The keep is surrounded by a solid defence wall by bastions which, however, did not have any actual military function. The main seat of the Prussian "Albrecht line" was to embody the power and prosperity of its owners.

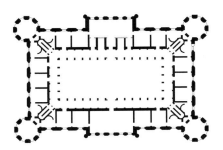

After the disappointing failure of the great Acropolis project, Schinkel was indeed to be granted the possibility of building a "fairytale castle" towards the end of his life. The client was Princess Marianne, one of the Dutch king's daughters. She had been married to Prussian Prince Albrecht since 1830. Schinkel had rebuilt the palace of the newly married couple in Berlin to their great satisfaction. In 1837, Marianne inherited from her mother the Silesian estate in Kamenz at the foot of the Sudeten Mountains. She was so impressed by its scenic location that she requested a great castle to be built there. Kamenz would not serve as a summer retreat only, but also as the main residence for the Albrecht line in the Hohenzollern family. Such a plan was not out of the ordinary since various dignitaries and members of the Prussian royal household already owned stately castles in the surrounding locations.

Schinkel received the commission to design the plans for Kamenz Castle in 1838. After visiting Silesia, he prepared complete designs for a Gothic-romantic construction complex of enormous proportions. Schinkel planned the castle as a brick building of a well-fortified character. Towers, merlons, perimeter walls and bastions gave the building a serious note. Although Schinkel used colourfully glazed brick as he had in the Academy of Architecture before, the fortress-like building and the inner courtyards still seemed dark and foreboding. The construction forms used gave the castle an awe-inspiring air. Unlike other projects such as the cheerfully romantic neo-Gothic design that Schinkel used for Babelsberg Castle near Potsdam in its asymmetrical, picturesque grouping, Kamenz Castle had a strictly symmetrical construction. The main façade seemed intimidating with its two flanking solid round towers and plain brick surfaces. Narrow towers framed the central risalite over which the royal coat of arms was placed.

An entrance ramp vaulted by a two-nave hall serving at the same time as a terrace stretched across the whole main front of the castle. Splendid open stairs led up to the state rooms on the main floor. The interior of each room was arranged in the splendour of the medieval period; East Prussian castles of the Teutonic Order, such as the famous Marienburg Castle, served as models. The interior was damaged, but restoration has started.

The castle was begun in 1840. Since Schinkel had already started showing serious symptoms of illness during the design phase, his pupil Martius was entrusted with the construction work. Martius was in charge of the building until its completion in 1873; some individual amendments to Schinkel's plans were made after his death.

1839·Church in Petzow
Brandenburg

Outside view.
On the highest elevation of the Petzow estate on Lake Schwielow, the small village church rises as a landscape feature that could be seen from far away. The tower was planned from the beginning as a vantage point.

One of the last buildings that Schinkel designed before his serious illness was the small village church in Petzow. Along with its landscaped garden designed by Peter Joseph Lenné, a reconstruction of the manor house in the Tudor Gothic style carried out in the 1820s, and architecturally ambitious residential buildings, the estate located on Lake Schwielow near Potsdam still exists as a Gesamtkunstwerk ("single work of art"). Schinkel probably also supplied the designs for the castle and some of the residential buildings. The squire of the manor, Carl Friedrich August von Kaehne, had the firm intention of completing the estate with the construction of a church in 1839. The church, located on a hill set into the countryside and intended for the 200 parishioners of the manor, formed the highlight—in the true sense of the word—of the estate. Although the construction task was not actually particularly important, the squire was still anxious to have his property designed as a stately landscape garden. His aims also corresponded to the artistic targets of the Prussian crown prince, who himself encouraged and commissioned similar estates in districts around Potsdam. Schinkel's design resulted in a rural church that was small in size, but still exceptionally ambitious as a building. The squire finally succeeded in having Schinkel's design approved despite resistance form the budget-conscious authorities.

Schinkel intended to build a church and tower separately and to connect them by an arch on which one could walk. Similar plans had already been prepared for the construction of the far more urban Gertraudenkirche (Church of St Gertrude) in Berlin in 1819. Schinkel had also revived his architectural idea from his design of "a small church with a tower" from 1828, and applied the idea to a small building. The long preliminary planning process could finally be implemented in Petzow. Schinkel not only achieved a marvellous picturesque effect in the church; the tower also served as a vantage point to view the surroundings, and could be accessed regardless of whether the church was open. The simple apse projecting outwards also gave the otherwise simple chapel particular dignity.

The interior design was modest but effective. Ornamental brickwork decoratively covered the floor; the altar niche and ceiling were painted in dignified tones and the wooden-beam ceiling was a simple but tasteful construction.

The Petzow church proves that Schinkel, who had planned and examined hundreds of church projects as a construction official and prepared magnificent designs for palaces and cathedrals, had not at all lost the ability to achieve a great effect with limited resources in smaller buildings.

Opposite page:
Interior to the east.
The interior of the village church in Petzow is impressive in its simple but harmonious design. The choice of colour and the skilfully arranged brick flooring gave the room an atmosphere of solemn dignity.

Life and Work

Karl Friedrich Schinkel at the age of 23.
Painting by J. Rößler, 1803.

Opposite page:
Portrait of Karl Friedrich Schinkel.
Painting by Carl Friedrich Ludwig Schmid.

1781 ▶ April 13th: born in Neu-Ruppin.

1787 ▶ City fire in Neu-Ruppin; father dies.

1792–94 ▶ Schinkel attends grammar school ("Gymnasium") in Neu-Ruppin

1794 ▶ The Schinkel family moves to Berlin. Schinkel attends "Zum Grauen Kloster" grammar school

1797 ▶ Friedrich Gilly's design for the monument to Frederick II at the Academy exhibition gives Schinkel the impetus to become an architect.

1798 ▶ Schinkel leaves grammar school and becomes a pupil of David and Friedrich Gilly – a close friendship with Friedrich develops.

1799 ▶ Studies at the newly founded Academy of Architecture.

1800 ▶ Schinkel's mother dies. Friedrich Gilly dies. He continues and completes Gilly's architectural projects, and leaves the academy. The first building of his own is the Pamona Temple on Pfingstberg hill.

1802 ▶ Reconstruction of Buckow Castle; designs for Köstritz Castle reconstruction (not realised). Stage set design for "Iphigenie in Aulis" by Gluck (not realised)

1803 ▶ Study visit to Italy (via Dresden, Prague, Vienna, Trieste). Extensive drawing activity; developed friendship with W. von Humboldt and J. A. Koch in Rome

1804 ▶ Stay in Rome, Naples, and at Sicily. Plans publication on medieval architecture in Italy (never realised); landscape drawings, first oil painting.

1805 ▶ Return home via Florence, Milan, Paris, Strasbourg, and Weimar. Schinkel is to create most of his paintings up to 1815.

1806 ▶ Architectural activity in Prussia has come to a standstill since the defeat against Napoleon. Schinkel begins work on the Diorama and meets Susanne Berger, his future wife.

1808 ▶ Schinkel's Palermo panorama receives public acclaim; he designs the Höhler and Feiner ceramics factory.

1809 ▶ Schinkel marries Susanne Berger. He applies for a position in the civil service as an architect. His first lithographs are created; he makes contact with the royal family through his Diorama exhibition. Schinkel is commissioned to

Portrait of Schinkel's wife, Susanne, around 1810–13.

design fittings in the crown princes' palais (realised from 1810 to 1811).

1810 ► Daughter Marie is born. Schinkel is appointed Geheimer Oberbauassessor, a senior position in the civil service for architecture; designs the Mausoleum for Queen Louise (not realised).

1811 ► Daughter Susanne is born. He is granted full membership of the Royal Arts Academy. Louise memorial at Gransee.

1812 ► Designs for singing academy (not realised); Diorama: Moscow's Great Fire

1813 ► Son Raphael is born. Schinkel joins conscription army but stays in Berlin; designs the "Iron Cross." Painting: "Cathedral on the River" (Kathedrale am Strom). Napoleon is defeated.

1814 ► First oil painting exhibition. Schinkel plans the Memorial Cathedral to the Wars of Liberation; festive decoration for the victory celebration at Brandenburg Gate.

1815 ► He is promoted to senior building official. Assessment "Fundamentals of the Upkeep of Old Monuments and Artefacts of our Country" (Grundsätze zur Erhaltung alter Denkmäler und Altertümer unseres Landes). Stage sets for the "Magic Flute". First performance on January 18th, 1816. By 1834, Schinkel has created the decoration for around 40 plays.

1816 ► Schinkel plans the New Guardhouse (Neue Wache) on Unter den Linden boulevard (construction carried out up to 1818); assessment for the completion of Cologne Cathedral.

1817 ► Interior reconstruction of Berlin Cathedral (outer construction carried out up to 1822). First city building map for redesigning the Berlin city centre is developed.

1818 ► Reconstruction of the Berlin National Theatre (up to 1821); design for the Kreuzberg monument (up to 1821). Designs state architecture reform.

1819 ► First volume of the "Collection of Architectural Designs" (Sammlung Architektonischer Entwürfe, published until 1840). Designs Castle Bridge (Schlossbrücke; construction carried out up to 1824) and the church on Spittelmarkt (not realised).

1820 ► Schinkel is appointed professor of architecture without teaching activity; reconstructs Tegel Castle (construction carried out up to 1824) and Neuhardenberg Castle (carried out up to 1823)

1821 ► Plans for Friedrichswerder Church (constructed between 1824 and 1831). Starts work on "Examples for Manufacturers and Craftsmen" (Vorbilder für Fabrikanten und Handwerker, published until 1837).

1822 ► Daughter Elisabeth is born. Designs for the Museum at the Pleasure Garden (carried out up to 1830). First design for monument to Frederick II (not realised). Construction of Antonin hunting lodge (carried out up to 1824).

1823 ► Plan for Leipziger Platz and Potsdam Gate. New assessment for Cologne Cathedral (construction continues in 1826).

1824 ► Second journey to Italy. Reconstruction of Glienicke Castle and Casino (up to 1827); Cavaliers' house on Pfaueninsel (Peacock island; up to 1826)

The artist's children, 1820.

1825 ► Granted honorary membership of the Accademia di San Luca in Rome. Design of the Community House (Gesellschaftshaus) in Magdeburg (construction carried out up to 1829). Painting: "Glimpse of Greece's Golden Age".

1826 ► Journey to Paris and England. Design of the Neuer Packhof at the Kupfergraben castle moat. Design for St Nicholas' Church in Potsdam (construction carried out up to 1849).

1827 ► Design for a public department store on Unter den Linden (not realised); design of the "normal church" as a model for smaller rural church buildings.

1828 ► Design for Redern Palace on Pariser Platz (carried out up to 1830).

1829 ► Designs for the reconstruction of Prince Albert's Palace on Wilhelmstrasse (construction carried out up to 1833). Design of the court gardener's house at Sanssouci (carried out up to 1830)

1830 ► Appointment as Geheimer Oberbaudirektor, senior director of the royal building authority, head of the Oberbaudeputation. Design for the Jenisch country seat near Hamburg (altered in realisation, construction carried out up to 1833)

1831 ► Design of the Academy of Architecture (realisation up to 1836, destroyed) and the main guardhouse in Dresden (construction carried out up to 1833).

1832 ► Design for four churches in Berlin's suburbs: St Elizabeth's, St Paul's, St John's and the Church of Nazareth (construction carried out up to 1835)

1833 ► Design of the Roman Bath in Sanssouci (construction carried out up to 1836), design of Babelsberg Castle (construction carried out up to 1835)

1834 ► Suggestion for a nature park. Designs for a Royal Palace on the Acropolis for the Greek King Otto of Bavaria (not realised).

1835 ► Design of a prince's residence, last chapter of the architectural textbook (which remained unfinished)

1836 ► Designs for the reconstruction of castle and church in Erdmannsdorf (construction carried out up to 1838 and 1840, respectively)

1837 ► Design for Werky Castle near Vilna. Design of Gotha theatre (completed with alterations in 1840)

1838 ► Appointed Oberlandesbaudirektor, senior director of the national building authority. Design for Kamenz Castle (completed with alterations in 1873). Designs for Orianda Castle in the Crimea (not realised). The first monograph on Schinkel, written by Franz Kugler.

1839 ► Assessment of the Berlin abbey church and St Nicholas' Church in Spandau. The first symptoms of paralysis appear.

1840 ► Plans for a new, larger exhibition of panoramas. September 9th: first stroke, and onset of almost constant unconsciousness.

1841 ► October 9th: Schinkel dies in his living quarters at the Academy of Architecture.

1842 ► Schinkel's estate is acquired by King William IV, forming the basis of the Schinkel Museum constructed in 1844 in his former official residence.

Glienicke Castle	**Babelsberg Castle**
Berlin-Wannsee	Potsdam
Church	**Kamenz Castle**
Petzow	Poland
Charlottenhof Castle	**Royal Palace on the Acropolis**
Potsdam	Greece
Pomona Temple	**Orianda Castle/Yalta**
Potsdam	Ukraine

Berlin

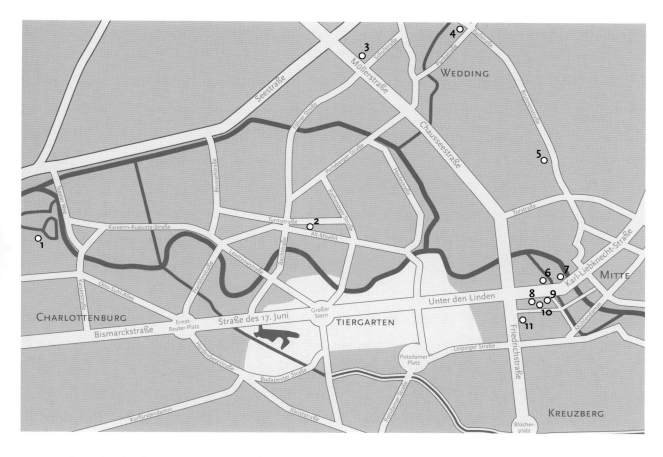

1. New Pavilion (Schinkelpavillon)
Charlottenburg Castle
2. St John's Church
Alt-Moabit 25
3. The Church of Nazareth
Leopoldplatz
4. St Paul's Church
Badstraße 50

5. St Elisabeth's Church
Invalidenstraße 3
6. New Guardhouse
Unter den Linden 4
7. Altes Museum
Lustgarten
8. Friedrichswerder Church
Werderscher Markt

9. Castle Bridge
Unter den Linden
10. Academy of Architecture
Werderscher Markt
11. National Theatre
Gendarmenmarkt

Bibliography

Credits

▶ Schinkel's complete oeuvre is being published in 22 volumes. The work is entitled: Karl Friedrich Schinkel: Life and Work, started by the Academy of Architecture in Berlin, continued by Paul Ortwin Rave, edited by Margarete Kühn.
This includes:
Peschken, Goerd: Das Architektonische Lehrbuch, Berlin/Munich 1979
Rave, Paul Ortwin: Berlin. Part I: Bauten für die Kunst, Kirchen und Denkmalpflege, Berlin 1942
Rave, Paul Ortwin: Berlin. Part II: Stadtbaupläne, Brücken, Straßen, Tore, Plätze, Berlin 1948
Rave, Paul Ortwin: Berlin. Part III: Bauten für die Wissenschaft, Verwaltung, Heer, Wohnbau und Denkmäler, Berlin 1962

▶ Bergdoll, Barry: Karl Friedrich Schinkel. Preußens berühmtester Baumeister, München 1994 (English title: Bergdoll, Barry: Karl Friedrich Schinkel. An Architecture for Prussia, New York 1994)
Bernhard Maaz (ed.): Die Friedrichswerdersche Kirche. Schinkels Werk, Wirkung und Welt, Berlin 2001
▶ Börsch-Supan, Helmut: Karl Friedrich Schinkel, Bühnenentwürfe/Stage Designs, Ernst und Sohn, Berlin 1990
▶ Forssman, Erik: Karl Friedrich Schinkel, Bauwerke und Baugedanken, Munich 1981
▶ Hedinger, Bärbel/Berger, Julia (eds.): Karl Friedrich Schinkel, Möbel und Interieur, Deutscher Kunstverlag, Munich/Berlin 2002
▶ Haus, Andreas: Karl Friedrich Schinkel als Künstler. Annäherung und Kommentar, Munich/Berlin 2001
▶ Philipp, Klaus Jan: Karl Friedrich Schinkel. Späte Projekte/Late Projects, Stuttgart/London 2000
▶ Schinkel, Karl Friedrich: Sammlung architektonischer Entwürfe – Collection of Architectural Designs (reprint), Chicago 1981
▶ Snodin, Michael (ed.): Karl Friedrich Schinkel. A Universal Man, New Haven/London 1991